Praise for

Secrets of the
ULTIMATE HUSBAND HUNTER

"Read, Ladies, and find The Secret to attracting men. Read further and find The Secret to finding the right man. Nancy Nichols gives us easy reading, fun and light-hearted, but a true bouquet of candid pointers on how to man hunt—woman style."

—Dr. Ben Johnson, featured teacher in the
New York Times **Bestseller** *The Secret*

"Brace yourself . . . read these gutsy words that will transform you into a confident, self-sufficient, alluring woman!"

—Jess Kennedy Williams, Author of *Heartbreak-Free Dating*

"Nancy's book has opened my eyes to relationships with men. I have discovered a new comfort level with them."

—Tracy Scott, Regional Cosmetics Consultant

"Nancy Nichols's book changed my life. After a recent divorce, I needed to look deep inside myself and figure out what I was doing wrong and what I could do to change the behavior. Not only did the book identify what I was doing wrong but it gave me great information on how I could correct it and move forward."

—Jami Hollingsworth, Retail Franchise Owner

Secrets

of the

ULTIMATE HUSBAND HUNTER

How to Attract Men, Enjoy Dating and
Recognize the Love Of Your Life

Nancy Nichols

 EPIPHANY IMPRINT

EPIPHANY IMPRINT, LLC
Email: info@epiphanyimprint.com
www.ultimatehusbandhunter.com

Disclaimer: This book is designed to provide accurate information with regard to the subject matter covered. It is sold with the understanding that the publisher and author are not engaged in rendering legal, psychological, or other professional advice. If expert assistance is required, the services of a competent professional person should be sought.

Names, locations and identifying characters of people in the book have been changed to protect the privacy of the individuals.

ISBN: 978-0-9795791-0-3

Library of Congress Control Number: 2007926982

Printed in the United States of America

This book is available for quantity discounts for bulk purchases. For information, please email info@epiphanyimprint.com.

Editor, Dawn Sachs

To my vibrant, beautiful daughter,
Krissy, whom I dearly love.

To my son, Roger,
thank you for your faith in me,
your continuous love and
support and your male wisdom.

Contents

About the Author   xi

Acknowledgments   xiii

Introduction   xv

My Story   xxi

PART ONE:
LOVE-ALL-MEN PHILOSOPHY

1   Starting Over—Again!   3

2   Wising Up   9

3   Turning Point   18

4   The Epiphany   24

PART TWO:
LOVE-ALL-MEN STRATEGIES

5   Tips, Tactics and Techniques That Attract Men   29

6   Attitude Adjustment   33

7   Approachable Spirit   37

8   Pre-Judging Appearances   44

9   Meeting New Men   51

10	Dating New Men	64
11	Keeping Men as Friends	73
12	Words to Say	84
13	Be a Giver—Not a Taker	92
14	Personal Ten Commandments	96
15	Code of Ethics	99

PART THREE:
THE SABOTEURS

16	Saboteurs of the Love-All-Men Spirit	103
17	Saboteur No. 1: I'm Fearful, I'm Mistrusting	106
18	Saboteur No. 2: I'm Picky, I'm Choosy	110
19	Saboteur No. 3: I'm Critical, I'm Opinionated	113

PART FOUR:
THE WELL-EQUIPPED WOMAN

20	Intro: Gearing Up	119
21	Discovering Self-Confidence	120
22	Honoring Your Intuition	125
23	Smile	131
24	Sprucing Up Your Curb Appeal	136
25	Taking Care of Yourself	145

PART FIVE:
AVOIDING THE PITFALLS OF DATING

26 Shooting Yourself in the Foot   151
27 Don't Be a Needa Man   154
28 Scaredy-Cat Girl   160
29 Good-Bye Needa Man and Scaredy-Cat Girl   165
30 Survival Tips for the Needy, Fearful Woman   171
31 Don't Be Giving the Squirrel Away   175
32 Loss of Mystery   185
33 Never Hunt a Dead Animal   193
34 Recognizing When to Move On   198

PART SIX
90-DAY DATING PRINCIPLES

35 90-Day Dating Plan   207
36 Fast Track to Finding the Right Man   212
37 90-Day Hunting List   220
    Final Thoughts   233

    Appendix A: Memo to Men   236
    Appendix B: Recommended Reading   239
    Appendix C: Source Notes   243

PART FIVE:

About the Author

NANCY NICHOLS has been a professional businesswoman for over thirty years. Her background is in advertising, marketing and sales. Her latest position was as a regional business consultant, trainer and motivational speaker for a national skincare and cosmetics company. She has worked with women nationwide for the past fifteen years in the area of self-improvement. She previously owned the Before and After Image Consulting Company, performing corporate image seminars for professional business women. She was a columnist for a monthly Memphis magazine. Nancy Nichols left the cosmetics industry in 2006 to complete and promote her book, *Secrets of the Ultimate Husband Hunter.*

Nancy Nichols is available for speaking engagements and can be contacted through her email at info@epiphanyimprint.com.

Acknowledgments

To those who believed in me and my book:

Phyllis, my longtime friend, who supported and encouraged me to complete my book; who introduced me to my new friends and incredible editing team in Houston, TX.

Dawn, what a wonderful discovery you were; thank you for your friendship, your creative and knowledgeable contributions and for joining me as editor of my book.

Thank you to my early readers, Peggy Jennings, Ruth Caples, Kay Clark, Jami Hollingsworth, Barbara Lyons, Ann McMains, Tracy Scott, Gail Tynes, Barbara Van Dyke and Shelia Wilson who took time out of their busy lives to express their interest and support in my book.

Thanks to Kim Coffman for my fabulous author photograph.

Introduction

Who is the Ultimate Husband Hunter?

I know what you're thinking. *Ultimate Husband Hunter!* She sounds like a premeditating, self-serving opportunist who uses her calculating trickery and seductive ways to snag an unsuspecting man for her next expensive meal, a diamond tennis bracelet and the big house-on-the hill. Yes, these women do exist and they are a deadly force to be reckoned with by any man. But, I assure you, the *Ultimate Husband Hunter*, as depicted in this book, is quite the opposite of a woman who selfishly hunts for her trophy husband.

The prospects of dating, love and a lasting relationship can at times seem *unattainable*. Dating is a confusing, and often disappointing process. Love is an unpredictable emotion. Men are perplexing, and a loving, reliable relationship seems less possible with each passing year. No wonder the bookstore shelves are lined with relationship advice.

♥

This is the true story of how I discovered a dating and relationship concept so profound . . . so sensible and easy to apply . . . that it altered the course of my life. In the beginning it was a "means to an end" . . . to attract men and the dates they could offer. *Surprisingly,* it was a conceptual twist that ultimately taught me to love, respect and value myself. The result was: I achieved a level of self-confidence, self-esteem and a sense of self-worth that I had never known before. I acquired the approachability that attracts the interest of *Quality Men*. This unique transformation is the *core product* of the *Secrets of the Ultimate Husband Hunter.*

Just who is the Ultimate Husband Hunter? She is a woman who has rid herself of the attitudes and behavior that have in the past run men off. Instead, she has learned to be open-minded about the men she meets and dates, and to appreciate and respect a variety of men. Subsequently, her accepting, affirming, approving presence now attracts their interest. And the more men she attracts . . . the more self-confident she becomes. The more self-confident she becomes . . . *THE MORE MEN SHE AGAIN ATTRACTS!*

It is the influence of a woman's smile, the enticement of her accepting, approachable spirit and the intrigue of her self-confidence that cause men to pursue her. And it is a woman's self-confidence that gives her the courage to raise her standards. This is the secret to her dating success.

The *Ultimate Husband Hunter* is looking for one very special man to be in her life. She decidedly avoids the dating and relationship mistakes of her past. She is cautious to avoid dysfunctional relationship entrapments in her future.

She defines the traits, qualities and characteristics that she wants and needs in her special man; someone who is capable of contributing to a supportive, loving, intimate, stable, long-term relationship. And then she waits. She selectively waits for the Right Man to come along.

The *Ultimate Husband Hunter* is the *Ultimate Woman* who is looking for her *Ultimate Man.*

Secrets of the *Ultimate Husband Hunter* is a true life dating discovery that became a compelling, inspiring self-improvement book. It is for women of all ages who are:

- *NEEDY, UNCERTAIN* and *INSECURE* with men
- *DISILLUSIONED* with the dating process
- *DISCOURAGED* with the prospect of finding a *QUALITY MAN*
- Continually *DATING* and *COMMITTING* to the *WRONG MAN*

You Will Learn How to Date With A Purpose!

Within the pages of this book you will learn how to:

- *ATTRACT* the sincere interest of *QUALITY MEN*—and *KEEP* it
- Truly *ENJOY* the dating process
- *STOP* the *BAD CHOICES* of your past
- *AVOID DYSFUNCTIONAL RELATIONSHIPS* in your future
- *ULTIMATELY* find, attract and "capture" the heart of your *DREAM MAN*

You will discover the principles that encourage a *Quality Man* to pursue a woman. You will learn how to take the focus off of your insecurities and enjoy dating a wider range of men. You will learn how to meet, date and ultimately find the *Love-of-Your-Life*.

You Will Learn How to Be an Attractive, Confident, Self-Reliant Woman!

It is the influence of a woman's accepting, welcoming presence that captures the interest of men. It is the intrigue of her self-confidence that draws men toward her. It is her approachable spirit which gives men the courage to pursue her. And once a man is in her presence, it is her affirming, respectful manner that invites him to stay.

You will learn how to project an aura of attractiveness, confidence and friendliness that captures the interest, admiration and respect of *Quality Men*.

You Will Learn How to Correct Negative Dating and Relationship Behavior!

If you *seriously* want to meet, attract and be with a wonderful man, you must take an honest look at the counter-productive attitudes and behavior that continually sabotage your dating and relationship opportunities. It is the negative attitudes about dating, men and life in general, that destroy a woman's confidence, femininity and self-esteem—along with her chances of meeting the kind of man she really wants in her life.

Every action produces a result. To change the result, you must change the action. My book will help you to identify and correct the bad attitudes, behavior and actions that are known to run men off.

You Will Learn How to Avoid Involvement With the Wrong Man!

The *Ultimate Husband Hunter* is looking for a very special man, one who is worthy of her love, affection and loyalty, and with whom she can build a secure future. To be with that man, she knows that she must carefully avoid emotional involvement with the *Wrong Man* . . . a man who is incapable, or unwillingly, to participate in a healthy relationship. And just when she least expects it . . . mysteriously . . . magically . . . the *Love-of-Her-Life* appears right before her husband hunting eyes.

Secrets of the Ultimate Husband Hunter will help you attain the love, respect and happiness you so richly deserve. It is a *go-get-em'girl* book that will empower you with the influential dating attitudes, alluring behavior and take-charge actions that will increase your self-reliance, self-esteem and self-confidence with men. The three "selves" that every single woman needs in today's dating arena.

My Story

The culmination of one's life is the sum total of the choices one makes in a lifetime. The life that I have lived has given me the words to write this book.

I am a woman who has struggled for most of my life with dating difficulties and relationship issues. I have always wanted to have a loving, caring, supportive man in my life . . . but couldn't seem to get one. I've always wanted to share my love and affection with the Right Man . . . but I seemed to continually waste my efforts on the Wrong Man. My life has been a morbid merry-go-round ride of dating frustrations and relationship disappointments that seem to have no end.

I asked myself, "Why am I unable to attract the interest of a Quality Man?" "Why do I continually commit to relationships that are emotionally, financially, even sometimes, physically harmful to me?" And "Why, when I escape one hurtful, harmful relationship, do I willingly repeat the same awful experience—again?" *Why—Why—Why* do I do this?

Most importantly, I wanted to know, "How do some women intuitively know how to get the attention, respect, and a relationship commitment from a Quality Man?" *How—How—How,* indeed, do women do this?

Thirty years of dating disappointments and relationship failures had taken its toll on me. I was looking for answers.

I was not born with, nor did I ever learn, good dating and relationship skills. My life's quest was to understand:

- What is the secret that attracts the interest of Quality Men?
- What am I doing that continually sabotages my dating and relationships efforts?
- Why do I repeatedly commit to men who are wrong for me?

For two decades I had worked on my relationship problems and personal growth. I read a plethora of self-improvement and relationship books. I was counseled by numerous psychologists. I strove to develop my spirituality. I observed my skillful girl-friends as they attracted men, hoping to absorb some small tidbit of relationship knowledge. I talked with hundreds of women who were also looking for solutions to this universal problem. Unfortunately . . . nothing seemed to work. I could not master the dating scene, nor could I overcome my penchant for dysfunctional men.

Then one day, quite unexpectedly, I discovered something that I had never read nor heard before. It was a dating and relationship concept so profound . . . so sensible . . . so easy to apply . . . it shook my world and altered the course of my life.

I named it the *"Love-All-Men" Philosophy,* which succinctly means, "give all men a chance."

Sounds mundane, doesn't it? Commonplace? Un-fantastic? Something that every woman should know, *right?* How can "give all men a chance" possibly improve my dating and relationship skills?

Take a look at the following significant chain of events.

In the beginning I set out to discover the attraction principles that entice a man to pursue a woman. I used my *"Love-All-Men"* dating strategy to attract men and I deliberately dated a wider range of men with the hope of finding, even marrying, the *Love-of-My-Life*. As I dug deeper and deeper into my relationship difficulties, I realized that it was my close-minded, judgmental attitude that was at the root of my difficulties with men. I went to work.

1. To attract men, I had to correct my judgmental, counter-productive style of relating. I conditioned myself to be more open-minded about the men I met and dated. I strove to "give all men a chance" to reveal their best qualities.

2. I altered my agenda from wanting and needing a man's approval . . . to accepting, valuing and appreciating a wider range of men. Not just the good-looking, successful ones but men who were less attractive, less successful, less outgoing . . . men that many women would have overlooked or rejected.

3. Surprisingly, it was this new approach to men which inspired my new warm, welcoming presence. I found that not only could I attract a man's interest, I could keep his interest with my accepting, affirming attitude, and would ultimately gain his admiration and respect.

4. Soon a variety of men were pursuing me. Quality men were showing a sincere interest in me which, in turn, bolstered my self-confidence and self-worth . . . all of which *attracted the interest of more Quality Men.*

5. Finally, it was my increased level of self-confidence which inspired me to raise my personal standards. And now only a *Quality Man* will do.

Surreal! It's the only word that can describe what I was feeling at the time. I discovered that the more men I affirmed, flattered and respected . . . *the more men I attracted.* The more men I attracted . . . *the more confident I became.* And the more confident I became . . . *Hallelujah! Praise the Lord! Amen!* . . . *the more Quality Men I attracted!*

For thirty years self-criticism had caused me to unknowingly project an aloof, sometimes pretentious . . . sometimes rejecting appearance to those around me. It was the *Love-All-Men Philosophy* that opened my eyes to my judgmental nature. The crowning reward was when I ceased criticizing others, I soon stopped criticizing and doubting myself. When I began to accept, respect and honor men, I also learned to accept, respect and honor myself.

What was the answer to all my relationship problems? It was this: To attract the *Right Man* . . . I first had to be the *Right Woman.*

Astoundingly the *Love-All-Men Dating Philosophy* altered the course my life, improved the quality of my girlfriends' lives, and became the philosophical foundation for my book, *Secrets of the Ultimate Husband Hunter.*

My editor asked me, "How does one learn to accept oneself?"

In the midst of writing my book and practicing my *"Love-All-Men" Dating Philosophy,* I read a book that told me: I was created for a special purpose. I was born with special talents, and my life was intended to have special meaning.

If this is true, then others must exist for a special reason *as well* . . . so who am I to criticize the uniqueness of others . . . and who are they to criticize and judge me? It was this inspiring message that helped me to be more mindful of others, as well as to forgive and accept my imperfections and appreciate my uniqueness.

My new creed became: Everyone has worth. I will no longer criticize the shortcomings of others. I will no longer allow others to criticize and judge me. Most importantly, I will no longer criticize and demean myself. And just like that . . . overnight . . . my negative attitude gave way to self-love and an understanding and compassion for others. I learned to accept myself. I learned to accept others. I learned to "give all men a chance." It is the direct path to finding and being with a Quality Man.

I am not a psychologist, a radio or TV personality, or the wife of a well-known personality. My credentials for writing my book are: I have lived the majority of my life as an insecure, confused and unhappy woman. My relationship Ph.D. is pain, hurt and dysfunction. I have felt the same intense unhappiness, desperation and emotional pain, associated with failed relationships that you, or one of your girlfriends may be feeling at this very moment. I learned how to be an attractive and confident woman, master the dating process, and to recognize the Love-of-My-Life—*the hard way!*

There are many informative and inspiring self-help books available for today's single woman. I know, because I have read and learned from the majority of them. That's why I am confident in saying, that the results that you will receive from my book can have a *profound effect on your relationships*. It happened for me . . . and it can happen for you.

Part One

Love-All-Men Philosophy

> "The Happiness of Your Life Depends on the
> Quality of Your Thoughts."
>
> —Anonymous

Starting Over–Again!

I have wondered all my life . . . are some women hard-wired at birth to know how-to-get a man—while other women are born clueless? Are some women destined to have effective relationship skills because their mothers pass on a predetermined "male-attraction" gene to their tiny newborn daughters? Or—are some women more fortunate than others because they were taught as young girls how to attract, charm and capture a fabulous husband? Someone please tell me . . .

Where Does This Relationship Talent Come From?

There is a mysterious, innate ability that some women seem to possess which gives them the uncanny capacity to attract the attention of men wherever they go. They have men smiling at them, talking to them and calling them for dates. They have men pursuing them, desiring them and wooing them toward serious relationships. And these women accomplish this . . . it seems . . . with little to no effort.

I know such a woman. Her name is Camille.

Camille knows how to get any man she wants. She captures the attention of men wherever she goes, be it the grocery store, the dry cleaners, the post office or the doctor's office. Everywhere men can be found . . . Camille attracts them all.

If we are at a party, all the men ask Camille to dance. When we are shopping, I frequently have to wait for her to finish an impromptu conversation with a man she has just met on the street. Wherever Camille goes, men gravitate toward her for conversation and attention. The trouble is—Camille is scheming, manipulating and self-serving. Nevertheless, there are powerful skills to be learned from this woman.

I, on the other hand, am a caring, thoughtful, loyal and affectionate woman. I want a fabulous man in my life to love, honor and care for . . . *but* I don't know how to attract him. I don't know how to keep a man's respect and interest, and I foolishly commit myself to the Wrong Man. This has been the unfortunate story of my life.

My life's dream has always been to marry my soul-mate, someone who would be my best friend, someone who would love me passionately and unconditionally.

When I married my husband, I thought we were going to be married forever. I thought we were going to grow old together and I would never be without a loving partner again until the day one of us died. Then one day, after living ten years with a man who ignored me and refused to work on our marital problems, I stepped between him and his television and announced, *"I have something to tell you that you're not going to want to hear. I want a divorce.*"

The heart-breaking truth was, the intense love I once felt for my husband had died. I had spent years struggling to make my unhappy marriage work, but to no avail. I couldn't make a whole relationship when only one of us showed up emotionally. It was with much sorrow and regret that I ended our marriage.

What's Wrong With Me?

I asked my "man-wise" friend Camille: "What's *wrong* with me? *Why* can't I find a wonderful, loving, considerate, caring man? *Why* am I unable to attract the attention of a *Quality Man*? And *why* do I *constantly* wind up with men who turn out to be *soooo very wrong* for me?"

To which Camille replied, "I just don't understand the stupid choices some women make in men. I have always set my standards so much higher when it comes to the men that I will date and the man that I will marry."

Camille continued, "When I was growing up my father was the most important person in my life. He was my mentor. Hc taught me how to understand men and he taught me what it took to get them. By the time I was 16-years-old I knew how to attract a man, flatter a man, and get him to spend his money on anything that my little heart desired.

As an adult it became my job to find a trophy husband . . . a man who, like my father, wanted to lavish me with his affection, attention and money. I grew up believing that a husband's job was to support me; I expected to live in a nice home, drive an expensive car, have a maid and go on fun vacations. These are my expectations because, after all, money can sometimes make an unbearable situation more tolerable. I can't do the love thing with a man who won't take care of me. Cocky? Maybe. Sensible? Absolutely."

I just can't understand it. What is it that men see in Camille? She's attractive, but she's not gorgeous. She doesn't have a job. She doesn't have money. What is she doing that always gets her this kind of attention? Men take her to the finest restaurants and best parties. Men give her flowers, furs and jewelry, and they sweep her away on fabulous vacations.

I must know—What is she doing that gets her this attention and admiration from men. But more importantly—Why am I unable to attract this kind of attention?

When it comes to men, it is very clear that Camille is highly opinionated, brazenly outspoken and unashamedly demanding. It's hard to believe that any man would be interested in her—but they are—and there are many. Obviously there was something about her which caused men to stop, look and listen.

Do not misread what I am saying, for I in no way condone Camille's manipulating, self-serving behavior. My fascination with her was pointedly: *How does she attract the interest of so many men?* I wanted to know the secret of her magic allure. I wanted to know if I could learn to attract men as she does, without taking up her self-serving ways.

As a young girl, Camille's father gave her everything she ever wanted. As a young woman, he took care of the smallest details of her life and it was his protective, indulgent, compliant influence that unwittingly conditioned her to take advantage of every man that crossed her path. *However*, it was his paternal mentoring that also taught her to *Revere, Respect* and *Honor* herself as a woman. Camille grew up learning to demand respect, attention and financial support from a man. She grew up believing that she deserved the very best from life.

So why then, are so many men attracted to her? Although the adult Camille functioned, more or less as a male predator, it was the unconditional love and support of her father that taught her at a very young age to enjoy, value and appreciate the very essence of a man. Her father adored her and she, in turn, worshiped him. This relationship nurtured her self-confidence with men and taught her an acceptance and understanding of them. It was the foundation of how she would relate to all men—*for the rest of her life.*

Camille said to me: "I just love men. I love all of them. I love the way they smell, the way they look, the way they move. I love all shapes, sizes and ages of men. I love them because they are different from women. I love them, because as men, they are unique and interesting."

When I first heard Camille make this absurd declaration, I thought, *"She's cracked!"* It was repulsive and disagreeable to me to think I could love all men. Then I realized . . . she was serious—*dead serious!* She *did* love all men!

It was my moment of truth. I realized that Camille had the unique ability to look past a man's flaws and imperfections and appreciate him for the simple fact that he was a *man!*

Camille's early relationship with her father programmed her to consider men as a source of pleasure, entertainment and companionship. For her being with a man was an experience to be enjoyed rather than dreaded and avoided.

Re-Entering the Single-Dating World

The end of my marriage was a very difficult time for me. Even more frightening, however, was my re-entry into the dating world.

Camille and I continued to have many enlightening conversations on "how to attract and capture" a wonderful man, as well as how to avoid a relationship with the wrong man. As I listened to her theories, I began to examine my own beliefs. The beliefs I had about men and the beliefs I had about myself.

I thought, *"I'm smart, attractive and outgoing. I have a good job. And I am very available."* But deep inside I knew that there was something wrong because . . . I did not attract dates that easily. I found it difficult to attract men of quality. And even more disappointing was to go out with someone I liked, and not be asked out again.

I asked myself, "Could I have a counter-productive relationship style? Do I have a negative approach to men and the dating process? Could my personal shortcomings be responsible for my bad choices in men? And if all this is true . . . what can I do to change it?"

The time had come for me to start my life over—again.

Wising Up

2

*T*here I was . . . *again* . . . subjecting myself to the callous, combative dating world.

When I thought about going out to try to meet a man, I felt anxious and awkward. When I envisioned myself dating a new man, I felt weak-kneed and nauseous. When I considered my lack of confidence with men, I felt inadequate and self-conscious.

Then I thought about Camille, a woman who o-o-z-e-d boundless amounts of self-confidence with men. A woman who genuinely knew how to enjoy the company of a wide variety of men; a woman who knew how to get any man she wanted.

For me, meeting a man was an intimidating, perplexing event. *For Camille*, meeting a man was a stimulating adventure; learning about him was an intriguing challenge; understanding him was a mental triumph. For Camille men were a source of fun and entertainment, an opportunity for friendship and companionship, even a possible romantic connection for herself or a girlfriend. Camille loved to meet, talk to and learn everything she could about almost every man she met. This is what she meant when she said, "I love all men."

It was Camille's open-minded, projected, implied interest in men that drew men to her. It's what caused the "male moth" to fly *happily* into her flame.

I admit, I was deeply envious of Camille's ability to attract men, and although I strongly disapproved of the way she maneuvered men for her own personal gain, I couldn't help but covet her capacity to command a man's respect and admiration. If only I could achieve that same level of respect and attention from men. If only I could acquire her inner strength and self-confidence. If only I could inspire men to passionately pursue me in the same way . . . *without* sacrificing my sincere, caring nature. If only I knew and understood what Camille has known and understood about men all of her life.

Camille was always trying to fix up her cute, younger sister Kitty with her latest male discovery. One evening I listened to Camille and Kitty as they were discussing men and dating when Kitty said, "You should see some of the guys Camille wants me to go out with. It's ridiculous! The last guy was a squatty, little bald man wearing an awful red plaid shirt. And his idea of a great vacation was to wade out into the ocean to spear fish for his dinner. *No thanks!* My idea of a fabulous vacation is a chaise lounge, beach umbrella and a frozen peach Daiquiri. Honestly, I don't know what she saw in this man."

"He was adorable!" Camille sniped at her sister. "He was considerate. He was charming and funny. He was a plastic surgeon—for crying out loud! He would make a wonderful, loyal husband, and while this doting bald man was scaling fish for your dinner on his 100-foot yacht, you could be in downtown Nassau shopping at Gucci, Prada and Fendi. Honestly, if I wasn't already married . . . I'd be going out with him myself."

It was this one single, isolated conversation with Camille and her sister that was the rocket that shot off in my head and parted the clouds above. *Yes*—for Camille, men were a matter of features, benefits and deep pockets, and her biggest concern was how a man could contribute to her overall comfort, social status and financial security. With that said, Camille genuinely appreciates a man for his more important, lasting attributes.

Camille purposely looked past a man's receding hairline, bulging stomach, dumb jokes or bad clothing choices to place emphasis on his more notable qualities. She was defending the squatty, little bald man because she truly felt his outgoing personality, caring and generous nature, loyal character and stability were much more important than his middle-aged body and frightfully bad shirt. She saw this man as a worthwhile individual who could make some woman a wonderful husband and companion. This was Camille's definition of—*loving-all-men.*

Camille also learned never to underestimate any man. She understood that she might not enjoy the same things he does, *but* she tried to value the qualities of each man she met. For example, she could appreciate a man who was an avid antique car restorer, or a skydiver, or stamp collector, even an enthusiastic storm chaser . . . and although she did not personally enjoy his activities, she would neither criticize or judge him, nor reject him for pursuing his favorite interests. She would, instead, try to understand his unique personality. After all, Camille knew she might learn something from this man that could be beneficial to her in the future.

"I'm Friendly. I'm Approachable. You Can Talk to Me."

How does Camille capture the interest and attention of almost every man she meets? She projects an intriguing, spontaneous, nonverbal message that tells men that she *accepts and approves of them.* This is her "man-sonar" . . . an affirming, alluring unspoken signal that causes men to respond to her in a favorable, friendly manner. She acknowledges them with her eyes and offers a friendly *"hello."* Once they are in her presence, she holds their interest by verbally affirming them as interesting, worthwhile individuals.

Men seek Camille out because they feel good about themselves in her company.

What is it that Camille does that gains her the respect and admiration of so many men? She *loves all men* . . . not in the literal, physical sense, but rather in the sense that she approves and values each man she meets for his unique qualities. It is this open-minded approach which creates untold opportunities for her to attract, meet, evaluate and, consequently, find men who are worthy of her time and appreciation.

Camille once told me: "Appreciating a man is as natural as taking a breath of fresh air. When I look at a man, I see a masculine smile, big strong hands and the uniqueness of his intelligence. I can admire a man wearing an expensive pair of Italian leather oxfords and an Armani shirt—or a man in khaki cargo pants and worn-in loafers. I appreciate the mailman who brings my mail and the serviceman who fixes my refrigerator. I enjoy the young, cute ones because they remind me of my son. I admire the middle-aged ones for their wisdom and stability. I love the grand-

"Love-All-Men" is the snare that causes men to fall victim to a woman's charm.

fathers because they remind me of my patient, caring father. I'll dance with any man, I'll talk to any man, and I'll give him a portion of my time and attention while I dig a little deeper into his character and background. And why not? I'm not obligated to go home with him, and when the dance is over and the conversation has ended, I may have made another valuable contact."

The truth is—men aspire to be in Camille's company because she accepts, affirms and appreciates them—*first.* Sometimes in a verbal way. Sometimes in a non-verbal way. Either way, it is her open-minded, friendly presence that quietly and unwittingly says to men, *"I like you for who you are. You are safe talking to me. You can enjoy my company."*

The "Love-All-Men" Philosophy

I named it the *"Love-All-Men" Philosophy* because it deliberately "gives a man a chance" to prove himself worthy of a woman's interest. It is a compassionate approach to men that:

1. Deliberately investigates the possibilities of a man

2. Examines the information gathered about a man

3. And, with an unbiased mindset, appraises the quality of a man

It is a cognizant, open-minded disposition that forestalls the negative opinions, unfair judgments and unreasonable expectations which a woman usually makes during the first few critical minutes of meeting a man.

What are these negative opinions and unreasonable expectations?

They are the petty, condescending decisions that a woman makes about a man's appearance, clothing, automobile, occupation, home, family, friends, hobbies, food choices, pets—or any of his other personal preferences. They are the uninformed snap judgments she makes about a man's financial status, social position, intelligence or character. She prematurely labels a man to be undeserving of her time and attention—before she really knows who he is.

> WARNING! Although the *Love-All-Men Philosophy* consciously looks for, hopes for and anticipates favorable qualities in a man . . . it has zero tolerance for men-swine, men-vermin and men-lizards. If, at anytime, a man reveals undesirable attitudes or questionable behavior, a woman should quickly remove herself from his presence to continue her search for a more desirable man. Don't worry . . . men are like buses . . . there'll be another one along in 5 minutes!

The Love-All-Men Mindset Can Create the Opportunity for a Man and a Woman to Meet

A woman who makes a conscious effort to *Love-All-Men* soon finds herself extending pleasantries to men during the normal course of her day that previously would never have happened.

She compliments a man on his nice tie as she waits in line at the bank. She holds an elevator door open for a hurried businessman struggling with his luggage. She leaves an extra-nice tip and a scribbled thank-you note for her attentive waiter. Or perhaps, she offers to share her small table with a man standing in a crowded coffee shop. And—*voila*—she begins to attract the interest of a variety of *Quality Men*.

It's every woman's dream . . . to attract the attention and admiration of men. You're sitting in a restaurant and an attractive man deliberately smiles at you; a man at a party goes out of his way to get your phone number from the hostess. A man in church skillfully makes his way over to sit next to you, or the hotel's desk clerk volunteers to comp you a room upgrade as you check in. These spontaneous, unexpected occurrences of a man's regard are the direct and magical result of a woman's *Love-All-Men* mindset.

What Do You Mean—*Love-All-Men?*

At this point, you may be saying, *"What do you mean—Love-All-Men? I couldn't possibly Love-All-Men because I can't stand most of the ones I already know. They lie, they cheat and they don't call when they say they will. They hog the TV remote control, they bad-mouth my driving, they leave their hair in the vanity sink and their dirty underwear on the bathroom floor. How in the world can you suggest that a woman* **Love-All-Men?***"*

Believe me, I understand! This was my knee-jerk reaction, too. But my dismal history of dating disasters, dysfunctional relationships and failed marriages left me dismayed about men and the dating process. I was determined to find out: *"Why* do I have such a hard time attracting men? *Why* do I continually choose men who are bad for me? *How* do I manage to run off the good men? And *WHAT* could I have done differently?"

A Disapproving Spirit Attracts
Few Dating Options

I have always felt that it was difficult for me to attract a Quality Man. My life was a joyless, vicious cycle of wanting to be with a man, finding a man, dating a man . . . and then running him off with my negative, disapproving attitude.

Every time I met a man, my rejecting voice groaned, *"This one's too short, that one is overweight, this one's too skinny, he's a lunch-bucket worker, he doesn't know how to dress and this one . . . well, his jokes are bad, boring and stupid."* I thought I was being smart because I was prudent about the men with whom I would socialize. But the sad truth was, my disapproving spirit was running off the men I truly wanted to meet and date . . . and then I wound up feeling rejected, hurt and lonely, which served to intensify my low self-esteem and lack of confidence.

Sometimes a man, even the *Wrong Man* can ease the emotional pain that arises from loneliness, a broken relationship or the disappointments of dating. I suppose that's how the *Man-From-Hell* found his way into my life.

It had been two years since my divorce; I was fed up with the dating scene and tired of being by myself, which led me to settle for a relationship with a man whom I suspected of being dysfunctional.

Maury gave the word "dysfunctional" new meaning. Late one afternoon, after two months of dating, I got a small glimpse into his harmful drunken behavior. It was an obvious warning sign of the malicious conduct to come. But I was lonely, so I closed my eyes and became involved with a man who was much less than what I wanted and deserved. It didn't take long for Maury's true nature to explode. He berated and abused me and eventually he hit me.

I finally got rid of Maury a year later, but not before his alcoholic, abusive behavior severely damaged my self-worth, dignity and personal security. The good news? It was this horrific relationship that caused me to face the truth and seek help for my own dysfunctional attitudes and behavior.

❧ ♥ ☙

If We Are Lucky in Life, We Realize That Our Attitudes, Beliefs and Behavior Are Responsible for the Outcome of Our Lives.

Yes, my life had turned out quite differently from Camille's. Her supportive, loving father taught her poise and self-confidence with men. Whereas my father and his critical reprimands conditioned me to, in turn, be hyper-critical, cautious and mistrusting of *ALL* men. I grew up fearing a man's disapproval and rejection. As an adult I didn't understand men; I did not know how to accept them and I felt insecure and flawed in their presence.

I had been practicing counter-productive behavior for most of my adult life. It was not something that I knew I was doing; nonetheless, it caused me to project an aloof and unfriendly presence. Men were afraid to approach me, and when a man did show an interest, I was prone to prejudge and disqualify him before he had a chance to bring his best qualities to the table. I guess one could say, I was the *Grim Reaper of Dating* and I used both my hands to grip the sharp, deadly sword that butchered my chances of being with a *Quality Man.*

I believe I was one of the fortunate ones, because I realized that if I kept thinking, doing and saying the same old things . . . I would continue to keep getting the same dreadful results . . . *over and over and over again.* And for me the results were: No date offers. No follow-up offers. And no *Man-of-My-Dreams.*

Turning 3 Point

ove-All-Men? Could this be the turning point in my life regarding the way I feel about men? Could this be "the magical cure" for my dating and relationship difficulties? Could Love-All-Men reverse the negative influences of my past and create a new positive future for me, as well as for millions of other women? It was a mind-boggling concept that needed much consideration.

Then I realized . . . the answer to a charmed and wonderful life was right there in front me. I can achieve the happy, stable life I've never known. I can rid myself of the negative attitudes that have demeaned and controlled me all of my life. I can be the kind of woman I've always dreamt of being. I can find the Man-of-My-Dreams. It is incredibly simple . . . because all I have to do is . . . Love-All-Men!

I began to ponder my new *Love-All-Men Philosophy.*

A woman who *Loves-All-Men* genuinely looks for the best qualities and traits in a wide variety of men. She deliberately "gives all men a chance" to reveal their best attributes. The result is: Her accepting, approving, compassionate mindset sends forth an alluring spirit that attracts the attention of many Quality Men.

On the other hand—a woman can continue to harbor a bitching, fault-finding attitude that repels every man who happens to cross her path. It's a choice. Alluring Spirit? Or a critical, faultfinding attitude?

Good In—Bad Out.
An Affirming, Approving
Spirit Will Displace
a Disapproving,
Judgmental Attitude.

Novel Dating Approach

I decided to apply the radical *Love-All-Men* dating concept to my life.

Instead of concentrating on a man's flaws and failures . . . I would concentrate on his best qualities, personality traits and accomplishments. Rather than dispensing disapproving remarks, I would instead offer positive words of encouragement and respect. Instead of focusing on *my need* for a man's approval and acceptance, I would turn my attention and focus on *his* need for approval and acceptance.

I was not yet brave enough to throw myself into the competitive dating arena. I wanted men to ask me out . . . *but*, I was uncertain of how to attract a Quality Man. Nevertheless, I was anxious to try out my novel *Love-All-Men* dating plan. I needed a man with whom to practice my new skills. *Click!* Match.com.

Tom was my first encounter in the world of internet dating.
From his photo, I suspected in advance that he was not the

typical man with whom I would be instantly or physically attracted, yet, he was courteous, friendly and fun to talk to on the telephone. My new, deliberate, open mindset told me to go out with and learn more about this man. We arranged an introductory meeting at my favorite neighborhood restaurant, Yia Yia's.

When I arrived for my date with Tom, I was insecure and nervous. I was accustomed to worrying about, "Do I look okay?" "Is he going to like me? And, "Will I impress him enough for him to ask me for a second date?"

"STOP!" I yelled inside. "That's your old belittling, negative voice. Now I am Loving-All-Men and for the next sixty minutes my job is to take the focus off myself and instead focus on him. My strategy is to find something about him that is interesting and entertaining. My mission is to make Tom feel accepted, important and relaxed in my company."

And so I did.

Fifteen minutes into our date, I could see that Tom was greatly enjoying my new Love-All-Men Philosophy. I complimented him on his attractive denim jacket. I admired his courteous manners, laughed at his unusually dry wit and approved of his motorcycle interests. I commented on his successful career achievements and while he was talking, I looked him squarely in the eyes, smiled warmly and listened intently to everything he said.

As the evening progressed, Tom began to realize that I considered him a worthwhile individual. And as he looked at me across the table, he couldn't help but enjoy my company and mirror back an equally accepting, approving attitude.

Tom smiled, laughed, talked, and he asked me out for dinner for the following Saturday night.

As it turned out, Tom and I were not a perfect match and we did not progress to other dates, but my coming-out-party was a huge success. I discovered that my Love-All-Men mindset was a dynamic dating tool and a powerful affirmation of another human being. I found that by focusing on the things that I liked about Tom, I learned to like myself as well.

Now I was ready to take my *Love-All-Men* dating strategy out into the vast dating world.

I Called It the Love-All-Men Game

I re-entered the dating world as a new person, casting an aura of acceptance, encouragement and lightheartedness among single men. *"I love all men,"* I told myself. *"I love all men, I love all men, I love all men. Everyday and everywhere I go, I will strive to find value within the many men that cross my path. I will try to give the men I meet an opportunity to reveal their good qualities."*

Men Are Everywhere and Everywhere I Go, I Tell Myself, I "Love-All-Men."

And so I did . . . in the airport, in restaurants, at the car wash, at parties, in the workplace, at the post office . . . I made a concerted effort to consider the good traits and qualities of the men with whom I came in contact. In the hotel lobby I appreciated one man's tasteful choice in clothing. In the grocery store line I enjoyed an older gentleman for his humorous personality. In church I admired the man in the next pew as he boldly sang out a hymn. And I greatly admired the largest man in the gym for the laborious energy he exerted to getting himself in shape.

Sometimes I would smile at them. Sometimes I would give them a quick, "hello." More times than not, I would secretly acknowledge their special features and say to myself, *"I appreciate this man as a person. This man has value. This man is someone's loved one."*

It was a fabulous dating strategy. When I found myself sitting across from a not-so-hot date, staring at him as he talked, I would concentrate and tell myself, "I *Love-All-Men* and for this moment, I am going to appreciate this man. I am going to smile and listen intently to what he is saying, laugh at his humor and enjoy his intelligence. I will comment favorably on his selection of wine and the dinner entrée. And why shouldn't I? I'm not going to marry him and I may never want to talk to him again . . . but right now, for the time I am with him, I am going to look for a special quality in this man.

I met Dennis, quite by accident, at a neighborhood restaurant where my girlfriend Rochelle and I were enjoying dinner and conversation. As we were dining I couldn't help but notice a good-looking man casually studying me from a short distance away. I thought, this is a perfect opportunity for me to practice my new approach; I flashed him my friendly Love-All-Men smile. Startled, he sheepishly smiled back . . . and then looked away. Then he looked back at me. Again—I smiled. He stared. I smiled. He then closed the distance between us by asking from across the room, "Do I know you?"

"No, I don't think so," I replied sweetly.

His name was Dennis, a tall, handsome, sophisticated, unmarried, successful entrepreneur who somehow managed to get my phone number that night and later called me for multiple dates.

As I said . . . wherever I am . . . I can always find a man to appreciate and admire.

I had discovered a powerful antidote for the lifelong critical, judgmental influences that had poisoned my mind and affected my behavior. The antidote was quite simply to *Love-All-Men.*

Months passed and I realized there was something different about me. I felt witty, charming, flirtatious, and confident. I found myself in interesting conversations with all types of men—old ones, young ones, tall and short, fat and skinny, rich and poor, attractive, and not so attractive . . . conversations that previously would have never happened. It was becoming easier and easier for me to step out of my comfort zone and say, *"Hello, how are you?"* It wasn't a ploy or a come-on; there was no hidden agenda. It was just my pleasant acknowledgment that said, *"I'm likeable. I'm friendly"* and *"I like you as a person—whoever you are."*

Yes, indeed, there was something different in my life. Men were smiling at me; men were flirting with me. They were asking me out for dates and pursuing me for serious relationships. It was thrilling because I knew that men were finally appreciating me in the best possible way. I wanted to **shout**, **beat my chest** and **scream**: **"Look at me** *and look at all these* **men** *who are paying attention to me! Boy, oh boy, oh boy—do I LOVE all men!"*

The Epiphany

I am a *Love-All-Men* Woman. And if I can *Love-All-Men*—why not love all people? And if I can love all people—why in the world would I not love, respect and take care of myself?

"Why indeed?" I asked.

As a child I learned to doubt, criticize and condemn myself. As an adolescent, I never felt I had the treasured, unconditional love of my father and consequently, I spent the majority of my life craving the love, approval and acceptance of a man. Without my father's acceptance I never learned to accept, respect and love myself.

As an adult, striving for personal growth, I knew I needed approval, acceptance and respect to make my world work. But how could I acquire that which seemed so elusive and unattainable? Where could I find a dependable source of unconditional love, comfort and support? Then it happened . . . an epiphany so profound, it gripped my soul and altered the course of my life.

Loving-All-Men Teaches Self-Love

In the beginning, my mindset was if *Loving-All-Men* can make me an irresistible, desirable woman in a man's eye—*then bring it on.* It was a strategy I devised to attract men and the dates they could offer. I ceased criticizing men; I accepted them as they were, and began to date a wider range of men in my quest for a hidden man treasure.

My life began to change.

I continued to practice my *Love-All-Men* strategies of being accepting, approving and affirming, when suddenly I realized—I was applying the same standards to myself. I persisted in seeking the good and appreciating the average in men . . . when quite unexpectedly . . . I began to recognize my own good qualities. The surreal experience was that when I threw away the critical measuring stick I was using against men, I subconsciously threw away the fault-finding standards I had used on myself all my life.

But there was more . . . The more forgiving I was of a man's imperfections and short-comings, the less I criticized my own failures and weaknesses. And when I took the focus off *my need* for a man's approval and acceptance and, instead, *gave a man* my unconditional approval and acceptance, I overcame my need for his validation. Astonishingly, when I freely gave what I wanted most in life—I received better than what I gave.

> *When I Freely Gave My Unconditional Approval and Acceptance to a Man, I Stopped Needing His Constant Validation.*

Ironically, Loving-All-Men taught me to accept, love and respect myself.

I learned how to accept a wider variety of men. I learned to genuinely listen to a man and to be interested in his different facets. I learned that each man is special in his own unique way. I finally learned how to be "in the moment" of a man's world . . . and it was there, in *his* world, that I achieved a level of confidence I never knew before. Instead of being fearful and anxious in a man's presence, I was relaxed and self-assured. I was no longer afraid of saying the wrong thing. I no longer feared his rejection. I was no longer afraid to be the "real me."

Men ceased to be a threat to me. *Why?* Because my *Love-All-Men* attitude altered the focus of what *I* needed from a man.

My life was never the same again; I did not look at men through the same uber-critical eyes. I did not treat men the same. I did not think or behave like the same woman.

Men were now an opportunity for enjoyment and entertainment, friendship, or even romantic connection. Now I am a focused, confident, caring woman who knows what she wants in life and is unafraid to go for it.

Love-All-Men is a mindset that proclaims: *"To Love-All-Men, one must learn to love, value and appreciate all people. To Love-All-Men, one must learn to love, value and respect oneself."* Yes, this is the magical secret that helped me build a quality life. It's the secret that taught me how to attract Quality Men, enjoy dating and eventually recognize the Love-of-My-Life. These are the powerful healing *Secrets of the Ultimate Husband Hunter*.

Let the Safari Begin!

Part Two

Love-All-Men Strategies

"Change begins with the desire to change.
Truth surfaces with the search for truth,
and it may require both to attract a Quality Man."
—Nancy Nichols

Tips, Tactics and Techniques That Attract Men

*I*t's *amazing!* Young women spend years attending college to prepare themselves for the professional careers that will reward them with a stable, secure and happy future . . . and yet, an astounding majority of these women will miss out on one of life's greatest joys—*meeting and marrying the Right Man.* How can this be?

Mothers teach their daughters how to cook, sew and decorate a home. Women study to become lawyers, doctors and research scientists—*but* amazingly, there are no schools to teach women how to attract and date *Quality Men.* Unfortunately, most women will never acquire the skills they need to help them find a wonderful, devoted husband.

I ask you: Aside from a successful career, money in the bank and a closet full of shoes, what could possibly be more essential than knowing how to attract a *Quality Man?* What could be more important than finding and marrying the *Love-of-One's-Life?*

A Master's Degree in Man-Skills Is an Investment in Your Future

- The quality and quantity of men you meet and attract are in direct proportion to your efforts and relationship skills.

- It has less to do with how you look, and much more to do with what you know and do.

When a woman decides to succeed at her chosen profession she attends classes; she diligently studies her textbooks, and often, she interns before taking her new knowledge and skills into the business world. Likewise, if a woman hopes to succeed at finding the *Love-of-Her-Life* . . . but her relationship skills are inadequate . . . she must read the books, get professional counseling, observe, talk to and learn from her more skillful girlfriends, and even get advice from her guy friends. Dating is like any other profession; it takes savvy and skill to succeed in today's modern dating world.

If you are reading my book, this tells me that you are looking for the skills that will help you:

- Attract the romantic interest of a *Quality Man (QM)*.
- Understand and enjoy dating men.
- Select the *Right Man (RM)*.
- Avoid involvement with the *Wrong Man (WM)*.

No matter what your age is . . . it is never too late to learn how to send out the right signals which will attract the interest of a QM.

ം♥ം

Attracting, meeting and dating men is not a passive expedition. It is, in my opinion, an important life's mission.

Too many times a woman will languidly sit back and accept what life offers her. Louisa May Alcott wrote in *An Old-Fashioned Girl:* "The 'women who dare' are few; the women who 'stand and wait' are many." Stand and wait? *Not in my century!* I propose that a woman take a creative, active part in making her life happen—*in her favor*. I believe that it is every woman's divine right to enjoy a happy, secure, prosperous life and that, *girlfriends*, includes having a fabulous man in your life. Where to start? To meet, date and be with the Right Man—a woman must strive to be the Right Woman.

Change begins with the *desire* to change. Change begins with a *willingness to accept* the idea that, "I may be the one who is wrong," meaning . . . the attitude you have about men and dating may be at the very heart of your relationship problems. The only way to change that is to ditch the "faulty" beliefs you have carried with you for a lifetime.

Understand, I do not present the dating strategies in my book as a self-serving man-hunting ploy, but rather, I consider it to be the appropriate "bait" known to attract men.

My advice is simple, yet profound. Realistic. Achievable. I can show you how to be a friendly, confident, attractive woman to a wider range of men. I can cue you on how to correct the negative attitudes and behavior which, in the past, have proven to work against you. I can inspire you to genuinely enjoy dating men. But it will *only* happen if you want it too.

Give serious thought to my words, follow the advice in this book, and I promise you, your life will never be the same!

Remember—a timid, passive, uninformed church mouse will, in all likelihood, attract and settle for a nearby church rat.

Whereas, a proactive, confident, soaring nightingale is certain to *attract* and *fly away with* a magnificent eagle. You reap what you sow. Improve your dating and relationship skills and go after a *QM* . . . or keep saying and doing the same old counter-productive things, and settle for what you can get. *Rat? Eagle?* The choice is yours.

Attitude 6 Adjustment

*T*here is one thing that every experienced hunter understands: *"Ya' can't ketch an animal if ya' ain't usin' the rite bait."* The same holds true in husband hunting. If a man doesn't recognize some desirable trait in a woman . . . he is just not going to be interested in anything else she has to offer.

But let's be realistic! Changing negative feelings and attitudes that took a lifetime to develop—*is not that easy*. Especially if our memories stem from a relationship with an absent, emotionally unavailable or abusive male role model. Indeed, it is difficult to rationalize the negative, painful feelings we have about the people and events that have deeply hurt us in the past.

When my father died fifteen years ago, I wept bitterly over his death because I knew that my opportunity to experience a closer relationship with him was forever gone. I never received my father's unconditional love, nor did I receive his support, mentoring or approval. I believe that the absence of a fatherly role-model in my life (one that would have taught me acceptance, trust and an understanding of men) fostered my low esteem and mistrust of *ALL* men.

The truth was that most men intimidated me because I did not understand them; I learned to hold them at a cautious arm's length because I was accustomed to the critical scolding of one man, an attitude that would later rob me of a chance at love.

A Bad Attitude Attracts Bad Men

It's not that a woman with a bad attitude can't get a man. She *can* and she *does*. The problem is that her bad attitude attracts bad men. *Conversely*—a healthy, upbeat, positive attitude attracts a mate who shares the same attitudes. So the woman with the nasty, negative attitude marries her kindred spirit, only to find herself years later divorcing her equally miserable husband.

A Good Man Will Not Stick Around to Endure a Nasty, Negative Attitude.

As an adult, I began to understand why I had such a difficult time attracting men. My critical upbringing conditioned me to project a negative attitude onto the men that crossed my path. My fear of men caused me to appear aloof, unfriendly and unapproachable.

A man will not risk having his big, male ego shot down by approaching a new woman, when all the signals tell him: "Beware, danger—bad attitude ahead!"

Move Over Bad Attitude

My *Love-All-Men Philosophy* was beginning to make more and more sense.

Thus far, my life was one big dating and relationship disaster. I ran off more men than I cared to admit. I wanted to believe that changing my negative attitudes could attract a *QM* and improve the quality of my life. It was becoming excruciatingly clear to me that if I ever hoped to improve my dating odds, I had to replace my negative, disapproving mindset with a positive, affirming attitude. Once again, I began to say my mantra . . . over and over again . . . *"I love all men, I love all men. I'm going to love all men and I'm going to rid myself of my unattractive, counter-productive, negative attitude."*

There I was, telling myself with each new man I met, *"I don't need or want anything from you. I am merely interested in discovering who you are."* I deliberately overlooked his small imperfections, and instead, appreciated him for his more important qualities. I gave each man an opportunity to reveal the traits that made him unique. It was liberating, somewhat empowering, as I began to relax, explore and enjoy the pleasure of a man's company. I smiled more easily. I offered sincere compliments. I listened more intently and I laughed effortlessly. Life was becoming a delicious smorgasbord of meaningful conversations with a wide variety of men.

A Shift in One's Attitude Can Cause a Visible Change in One's Physical Appearance.

❦

I was once a woman who was uncomfortable with and uncertain about men. I was unsure of how to attract men, and I felt flawed and awkward in their presence. I then realized, after living in the dark for 30 years, it was my negative, untrusting, fault-finding attitude that was at the root of all my dating and relationship difficulties.

And now? Men were spontaneously smiling at me wherever I went . . . or maybe I was smiling at them first. It really didn't matter because my positive, welcoming presence was attracting the favorable attention of *QM*. I couldn't wait to turn the page to see where my life was going.

Approachable Spirit

*T*here she is. It's Camille—reeling in another man. *What is it that she is doing to capture the attention of men wherever she goes? It is this* . . . she is accepting and appreciating them for who they are . . . *and they are eating it up!*

Camille would say to me, "Loving-All-Men is a habit. It's like brushing your teeth every morning . . . you don't think about it; you just get up and do it. You love 'em because they are men and because they are so very different from women. God must have thought we needed men or he wouldn't have created them, and if a woman doesn't feel that way—she doesn't need to be man-hunting."

Love-All-Men Is a Prerequisite To Developing an *Approachable* Spirit

It was as if a bolt of lightning had struck me. I thought, "I *understand!* I *get it!* I *know what I have to do!*" I have to *Love-All-Men* and I have to put my *Love-All-Men* plan into action. I have

to learn to relax, to enjoy, and to appreciate a wider range of men.
Much in the same way I would when I'm making new girlfriends;
I need to think of a man as someone nice to talk to. He is someone to learn from and
have to fun with. Some-
one to go new places
with and introduce me
to new people. Not
only will I enjoy dating
men, I will welcome the
opportunities for men
to date me, get to know me and enjoy my company . . . *until one
day* I discover that one special man with whom I want to share
my life. It was a simple, non-threatening agenda that wasn't really
an agenda at all.

An Approachable Spirit Upholds and Promotes the Love-All-Men Philosophy.

And so I did it . . . I went out into the world to meet, date
and enjoy a variety of wonderful men.

This was a very different dating experience for me. I was not
accustomed to men paying attention to me, flirting with me.
Nor was I accustomed to multiple men asking me for dates at the
same time. Even my girlfriend Annie noticed the attention I was
getting, and asked me, *"Damn girl, what are you doing? Where are
you finding all of these men?"*

Then I realized . . . there was something different about me,
my life and the way men were treating me.

Once I couldn't have attracted a *QM* with a 16-oz. T-bone
steak tied around my neck. And *now*—they were lining up to
take me to dinner. Men were seeking out my company and favor.
They were mirroring back the positive, accepting attitude they

saw in my expressions, behavior, and even, what they heard in my voice. I ask you, *what more could a girl ask for?*

An Approachable Spirit Is the Hook, Line and Sinker That Captures the Attention of Men

A woman's *Approachable Spirit* is one of the unique forces in life that empowers a man's natural instinct and desire to pursue a woman.

When a specific woman catches a man's interest, his natural inclination is to want to move towards and speak to that woman. *But*—if she seems aloof, unfriendly or unapproachable, he may fear rejection and, consequently, suppress his desire to meet her. His self-protective nature tells him, *"She's unattainable"* . . . and then he dismisses her, shrugs his shoulders and walks away.

A Woman's "Approachable Spirit" Overcomes a Man's Dating Insecurities.

By contrast—a woman's friendly, accessible presence can help a man overcome his fears. He will be more willing to take a chance if he believes that she will receive him in a warm and friendly manner. An *Approachable Spirit* is what gets a man off his seat, onto his feet, and moving in *Your* direction.

A woman's "Approachable Spirit" motivates a man to be the "Initiator" to a new relationship, in turn allowing the woman to fulfill her role as the "Responder."

An Accepting, Affirming, Approving Attitude Is the Cornerstone of an Approachable Spirit

At the core of an *Approachable Spirit* is an attitude that accepts different behavior, beliefs, opinions, appearances, lifestyles, religions and nationalities. It is a mindset that embraces variety and uniqueness. It is an attitude that appreciates individuality.

Regrettably, not all women are fortunate to have grown up in an environment that fostered an accepting, affirming mindset. Millions of women grew up absorbing constant criticism, disapproval and reprimands from parents, older siblings and other adult authority figures. Later as adults, many women are subjected to the berating, fault-finding remarks of a boyfriend or husband. The result: A woman absorbs the judgmental attitudes and believes the critical condemnations of others.

Camille was an accepting, approving person; it seemed women enjoyed her company as much as men did. She was always getting invitations from girlfriends to go to dinner, the movies or shopping. Looking back, I now understand it was because she was so non-judgmental and willing to overlook a girlfriend's mistakes or shortcomings. She did not condemn Cathy for her part in a failing marriage. She didn't criticize Joanne because she kept a dirty, messy house; or snub Linda when it took her days to return Camille's phone call. Come to think of it . . . I can't remember that she ever criticized anyone. She would just say, *"Oh, well— that's just the way they are."*

An "Approachable Spirit" is the Apex of a Woman's Feminine Nature. Men Recognize It. They Want It. They Need It. They are Compelled to Go After It.

A woman's *Approachable Spirit* is the powerful presence that attracts the curiosity, interest and attention of men. Men are intrigued by the poise and charm it exudes and are drawn to her friendly, alluring, yet non-threatening presence.

Each time Camille and I went to a party, I would stand back and marvel at how she could work a room full of men. But the truth was, that she wasn't "working" the room at all . . . *the room spontaneously came to her.* When Camille appeared on the scene, she released an aura of friendliness and approachability. Men left their wives

A Woman's "Approachable Spirit" Magnetically Attracts a Man's Interest and Attention.

and girlfriends side to say "hello" to her. They sought her out for conversation and company, and they would linger around her for as long as she would let them.

An Approachable Spirit Is not Anxious!

Before I found my *Approachable Spirit*, I had an anxious spirit. Anxious in the sense that I was desperately searching for a man. Anxious because I was secretly hoping that men would notice me and ask me out. Anxious if I were cornered by an unattractive man with his ho-hum conversation.

When I had an anxious spirit I was never content to just be in the moment with whomever, or wherever, I was. It was difficult for me to listen attentively to a man in whom I had no interest, because I was always afraid of missing an opportunity to meet a better man. My insincere, restless presence was a lethal "man-repellant."

Many Times an Anxious Spirit Arises From a Woman's Own Low Self-Esteem and Insecurity.

I set out to change my approach. Consciously I focused on developing an accepting, affirming, approving attitude for all men. Instead of worrying about attracting the "hottest" man in the room, I put my efforts into meeting and enjoying every man in the room. My new agenda was easy to execute: relax, greet, meet and give a wider range of men a moment of my cordial, undivided attention. *Presto, change-O* . . . my anxious spirit gave way to an intriguing, welcoming, confident presence, and the aura of that presence brought *QM* to me.

When I quit trying so hard to meet men . . .
they came to me.

- The **dating strategy** of an *Approachable Spirit* is to create opportunities to meet a variety of men.
- The **dating purpose** of an *Approachable Spirit* is to attract the attention and interest of men.

- The **dating goal** of an *Approachable Spirit* is to find, attract and capture the Love-of-One's-Life.

At the heart of an *Approachable Spirit* is a woman who has learned how to be delighted in the present, be content in the moment, and simply enjoy the man with whom she is talking. Not only will she have much more fun—she will attract more men in the process.

Pre-Judging &Appearances

*U*ltimate Husband Hunter Rule No. 1: *Never judge a man by his cover.*

You can't assume the worth of a man by the label in his suit or the car that he drives. You can't evaluate a man's sincerity, integrity or character by the length of his hair, the width of his waist or the size of his shoe. You can in no way judge a man based solely on outward appearances and for a woman to try to do so—*is a dumb move on her part.*

A woman who discounts and rejects a man purely on the basis of his looks and his possessions is only short-changing herself.

A man's unconventional, unfashionable, sometimes neglected outward appearance is not always an indication that he will lack the characteristics and integrity of a *QM*. Many times his most valuable traits are lurking just beneath a bad haircut, pudgy stomach, funny-looking eyeglasses or out-of-date clothing. It is a wise woman who will take time to look beyond a man's unpolished exterior for his best features. It is a wiser woman who will *quietly assist* a QM in sprucing up his appearance and improve his *minor* messy habits.

Now, am I recommending that a woman rescue some slob who doesn't have the good sense to practice good grooming habits? *Absolutely not!* Am I suggesting that a woman attempt to change a man on the inside? *POSITIVELY NOT!* If she tries to change him she will end up miserable and disappointed. But to discount a man because he is bald or short, his clothes are slightly wrinkled, he wears too many pens in his shirt pocket, or he snorts when he laughs—*is crazy!* It takes very little effort to help a man understand that it's time to ditch the aviator eyeglasses, trim the old mustache, buy a new suit and *please*, put the toilet seat down.

> *Until a woman walks in a man's shoes, rides shotgun in his golf cart and sleeps in his bed—she really doesn't know him.*

Peeling the Onion

A man is like an onion. He reveals himself one thin layer at a time. The only way to get to the core of a man's onion is to gently and skillfully peel back each illuminating layer.

It is a smart and focused woman who will explore a man's underlying nature to uncover his true intentions, attributes and temperament. Once she confirms that he possesses the qualities she feels are desirable for a solid long-term relationship, she can then decide whether or not to move forward. *However*—if she discovers that a man's flawed character or harmful relating style are the best he has to offer, she can quickly move on to greener pastures.

A man's beliefs, ambitions, behavioral patterns,
personality traits, moral characteristics, and even
idiosyncrasies, co-exist in the different levels
of his mind.

A Man-in-the-Rough Can Turn Out to Be The Man-of-Your-Dreams

My personal dating theory is: Give a man the benefit of a doubt; give him a chance to reveal his best qualities. I say, hope for the best, respect the average, but at the same time, acknowledge and avoid the unacceptable.

> *I once dated a man who kept fuzzy black covers, full of dog hairs, on the front seats of his very expensive automobile. It was a real turn-off. But this man exposed me to more fabulous art, new trendy restaurants and unique entertainment than I had ever experienced before. I just couldn't wear black slacks when I went out with him.*

On a more serious note:

Shelley grew up in California; she dated tall, muscular surfer boys, and then finally married one. When her three year marriage ended in divorce, she moved to Dallas with the hopes of meeting and marrying an urban cowboy.

In Dallas, Shelley had been dating various Mr. Tall, Dark and Handsomes when a girlfriend invited her to see ZZ Top at a local disco club. It was there that a friendly guy (not exactly her idea of a handsome urban cowboy) asked her to dance.

Michael was not Shelley's usual hottie, and she couldn't have been less interested at first, but when she discovered that he toured the world as a light and sound man for a major rock and roll band—her eyes lit up!

For the next three months, between Michael's international gigs, he wined, dined and danced Shelley to the point that tall, dark and handsome didn't matter anymore. Michael had won her heart with his enduring loyalty, affection, open communicative style, and a promise of a secure future together. She realized that, even though he did not possess the physical appearance of her preconceived macho man, he had more depth of character than any other man she had ever known.

Shelley decided to take a different relationship path. She accepted Michael's proposal; they got married and began a new life together. The following year, much to her surprise, and of his on volition, he gave up rock and roll and enrolled in medical school. After 23 years of marriage they have two wonderful children, a beautiful home, a loving and stable relationship and they expect to live happily ever after.

It just goes to show that you can't always judge a man by his "rock and roll cover."

A woman should maintain high dating standards. But when her standards are too high, she can become close-minded and rigid in her expectations.

I am not suggesting that a woman lower her standards. I am suggesting, however, that she be more tolerant and open-minded about the men she agrees to date. Many a woman has missed out on knowing a fabulous man because of her unreasonable, unrealistic requirements.

Rick, a 37-year-old single aircraft mechanic, met Glenda, a 31-year-old single dental assistant, while having his teeth cleaned. Rick was immediately attracted to Glenda, but it took two more visits to the dentist before he got the courage to ask her out. Glenda turned him down flat.

It seems that Rick fell short of Glenda's picture of the ideal man. He wasn't good-looking enough, tall or rich enough, and she considered him to be a blue collar worker.

Meanwhile, Angie, the 35-year-old accountant at the dentist's office witnessed Glenda's rude response to Rick. She thought he was kind of cute and decided to ask him out for lunch.

Angie, a divorced mother of a 4-year-old, was looking for a "family" man who would be considerate, fun-loving, communicative and stable. She sensed that Rick might be that man.

The short version of this story is . . . Rick turned out to be a Renaissance man with a golden heart. He loved to shop, gourmet cook, collect art and travel. He was affectionate, loyal, generous and outgoing. And if that wasn't enough to turn a gal's head, he piloted his own small airplane, owned a timeshare in Mexico and spoke fluent Spanish.

Making Snap Decisions Can Be a Lost Opportunity to Develop a Relationship With The Right Man.

It turns out that Rick, who was not quite handsome nor tall enough, was however, a very accomplished man whose new mission in life was to love, honor and care for Angie and her small daughter.

And Glenda, the woman with such demanding standards, was left pea-green with envy, and still very much alone.

Critical Selective Dating

Critical, judgmental, selective dating—it was something I had practiced all of my life. Instead of exploring an average looking man for his more enduring qualities, I was mesmerized by a good-looking man's flattering compliments, expensive dinners and flashy automobile. If a man were not attractive enough, if he didn't wear exactly the right clothes, if he didn't talk my talk, or walk my walk—he just didn't make it into my conversational circle. *How very sad!* Over the years my condescending, narrow-minded, judgmental attitude had robbed me of a wealth of male friends.

I knew I had to stop being critical and judgmental if I wanted to attract men. I knew that to attract the interest of a *Quality Man* I would have to be a *Quality Woman.*

Then I realized—I suffered at the hands of my own internal personal demon. It was a disapproving inner voice that judged, criticized and chastised me on a regular daily basis. It criticized me about the way I looked. It criticized me about the way I acted. It criticized me about the things I said and did. No wonder I could not accept the small flaws and imperfections in other people—*I couldn't even accept myself!*

The Magical Man-Key

I moved away from the critical, faultfinding attitude that seemed to sabotage all of my dating and relationship efforts. I tried to regard each man as a special individual, regardless of his age, appearance and position in life. It was this open mindset that made me realize that each man comes with his own unique set of qualities and possibilities. One man might become a supportive male friend, while another might be a great match for one of my girlfriends. And yet another man might turn out to be the *Man-of-My-Dreams* with whom to build a wonderful future.

It turned out to be a "magical man-key" opening the doors that had previously been slammed shut to meeting and dating QM.

A Word of Caution

It's smart for a woman to give a man the benefit of a doubt so she can learn more about him, *but*, if he is ungentlemanly or otherwise annoying, *DON'T* waste your precious time on him. Just get up, get out and remove yourself from his radar.

My friend Annette says, "You don't know why the good Lord puts men in our paths, but he does. And because he does, it's a woman's job to at least be nice to them long enough to find out who they are. But if you hear or see something you don't like, you should leave that man choking on a cloud of your pink dust!"

In the end, it is a woman's non-judgmental *Love-All-Men* attitude that releases her *Approachable Spirit*. It is her *Approachable Spirit* that puts her eyeball-to-eyeball with a wider selection of men. And, who knows? The next "average man" a woman accepts, affirms and approves of may turn out to be the *Love-of-Her-Life!*

Meeting New Men

Every day and everywhere a woman goes, she is in the midst of quality single men.

Each morning our husband hunter awakens to the face the possibilities of a brand new day. She sips her coffee, slips on a favorite outfit, and leaves home to go about her daily life. So busy is she with the interests and demands of her day that she barely notices the men who appear in her world, co-existing in the activities that surround her. Then, without a word, these men leave as quietly as they came.

During the course of a normal day a woman is continually presented with frequent, yet inconspicuous, opportunities to meet new men. An opportunity that could have developed into a *man-happening*, but didn't—because a negative-minded woman's unpleasant or unenthusiastic presence spoiled her chances. Here are a few words of advice for "Ms. Negativity":

When it comes to meeting men, a single woman's best ammunition is by far:

> (1) A Good Attitude
> (2) A Creative Mindset, and
> (3) A Tenacious Spirit.

No. 1—A Positive Man-Meeting Attitude Is a Necessity

Man-Meeting Attitude: It is a woman's overall good attitude that melts away the invisible barriers that keep men and women from meeting.

Robert, a 56-year-old divorced government auditor, said, "When a man walks into a room, he knows which women he can talk to, and which ones are going to shoot him down. Believe it or not—most men really are cowards. Even when a man thinks a woman wants him to speak to her, he is hesitant to make the first move. A small welcoming gesture from her can give him the courage to say, "hello."

A woman's welcoming smile, friendly laughter and courteous gestures can peak a man's curiosity.

There I was—single, dating and looking for ways to try out my new Love-All-Men Philosophy. Although I was apprehensive, I decided to attend a large Christmas charity event at the coliseum—all by myself. I was standing alone at an auction booth, content to be in the moment, when I happened to notice a man looking in my direction. Spontaneously I flashed him a warm and friendly smile, and then I returned my attention back to the auction items in front of me.

Long story short—Peter managed to work his way over to me, engage me in a conversation, and ask permission to call me for a dinner date. I dated this interesting man for almost two months.

The moral of the story is: I took control of my life, I ventured out into the world, and I took my positive Love-All-Men attitude with me. Was I nervous and uncertain? You betcha! But at the end of the night you couldn't peel me off the ceiling for all the good feelings I had about myself.

What if a woman is genuinely shy, mistrustful and uncertain, hindering her ability to meet men?

This is a valid question, many of us feel exactly the same way; however, when we use those feelings as a convincing and convenient excuse for not putting forth the time and effort that is necessary for meeting men, it then becomes a real problem.

Can she rectify her counterproductive men-tal block?

Absolutely! If a woman can put her own emotional needs on hold and, instead, concentrate on boosting a man's confidence and well-being, *she will be less likely to focus on her preconceived inadequacies.* The more she compliments and encour-

When a Woman Builds Up the Value of Another, She Contributes to Her Own Self-Worth.

ages a man to be self-confident in her presence, the more apt she is to be confident, poised and self-assured with him, as well.

No. 2 - Meeting New Men Requires Creativity

Man-Meeting Creativity: Think, say, be, and do something different. Develop a positive, friendly *man-meeting attitude*, take it to new places and position it in front of new eligible, single men.

Opportunities to meet men constantly surround a woman during the normal course of her day, that is *unless*, she works out of her home, has her groceries, drugs and dry-cleaning delivered, and her weekend existence is a sum total of internet surfing and TV reality shows. If this woman ever hopes to meet *her man* she will have to drag herself away from her isolating "zone of complacency" and place herself in new situations that offer new people and experiences. A *Dream-Man* cannot beat down a woman's door when he doesn't know her address.

Beverly is a good-looking, friendly, sensitive woman who says she doesn't know how to attract and meet men. So as her friend, I offered to coach her on how to do so. At first Beverly was thrilled with my offer, but the very next day she told me she didn't have time to date because of her job, housework, children, homework, charity obligations—blah, blah, blah, blah, blah! The truth was—Beverly was never asked on a date because it was just too much trouble for her to try to meet eligible men. She didn't want to get dressed up to go out. She didn't want to find a babysitter. But more importantly, she didn't want to set herself up for disappointment and rejection. So Beverly played it safe by sitting on the sidelines, all the while, complaining about her unhappy dateless existence.

Avoid Disappointments

Women who keep going to the same old places are continually going to keep seeing and meeting the same men. It's like visiting the boyfriend graveyard—the only men she is going to run into are her ex-boyfriends, ex-lovers and ex-husbands—or, *all three at the same time.* Just shoot me and get me out of my misery!

Likewise, a woman who goes out with the "high hopes" of meeting a new man, or running into a *man she already knows and likes,* is only setting herself up for disappointment and failure.

It was Friday night and I had just returned home from a week of working out of town. I was alone and bored, so I struck out for the neighborhood hangout, hoping to run into Don, whom I had been dating for several weeks and missed while I was away.

Big Mistake! I set myself up for a disappointing Friday night because not only did Don not show up, neither did any other datable guy.

Go Out With the Expectations of Meeting a Man and You Will See Your Evening Go From Bad to Worse.

What I should have done was focus on catching up with my girlfriends and guy pals and save my man-hunting efforts for a more inspiring, creative outing. I went out for the wrong reasons—full of hopes and expectations—and by the end of the evening, I wished I had just stayed home and cleaned out my refrigerator.

ᕤ ♥ ᕥ

Finding New Hunting Grounds

Go somewhere different: A new grocery store, restaurant, coffee shop, theater, dinner club, bookstore, church, singles' get-together or art gallery reception—the list is endless. Invite a girlfriend to explore these new social and recreational possibilities with you.

Do something different: Sit in a different church pew, go out on a different night, take up a new hobby, interest or skill. Allow your imagination to explore other activities that can enhance your life. To meet new men you need to think outside the box, because a box is exactly what it is; it consists of the four walls that hold *you in* and *new men out*.

New Places Have New Faces.

Consider Dating Services: Internet dating? *Absolutely!* The desire to meet one's perfect match has become today's big business. Contemporary single adults, young and old alike, are openly pursuing the innovative internet dating venues that put them in touch with other single men and women who are also looking for romance and commitment. Match.com, AmericanSingles.com, SeniorFriendFinder.com, EHarmony.com, Chemistry.com, Jdate.com and PersonalsYahoo.com are among the myriad of internet dating services that are only a "click" away.

In a recent survey of 38,912 singles, It's Just Lunch, a dating service, found that, "52% of single women and 48% of single men have used a dating service— compared to only 8% a decade ago."

Want to meet your man in the least amount of time? Try Speed Dating, Hurry Date, X-Factor Date and Blink Dating. These dating organizations invite groups of single men and women of similar ages to meet and interview one another in less than ten minutes. At the end of a dozen or more speed dating interviews, those with matched interests can set up a first date for another time.

Services offering lunch dates, Christian dates, Jewish dates, single parent dates, international dates, senior dates, lesbian and gay dates, and more are a huge part of today's single dating world. *Understand, I am neither recommending nor sponsoring these dating organizations or services*, but I am saying, that this is the 21st century and the new generation is more accepting and reliant on these services. It may be worth your investigation.

Caution: A woman can internet-date.com all day long, but if she is not taking a good attitude and dating skills with her, she will never attract the Right Man.

The Art of Approaching a Man

Thus far, I have said much on *how-to* attract the attention and interest of men. I've said that it is a woman's *Approachable Spirit* that gives a man the confidence he needs to step up to the plate. But what about a woman's sacred right to express her interest in a man by approaching him *first?*

When an RM recognizes he is in front of the Right Woman, he will do the right things to promote a relationship connection.

Years ago a wise counselor told me, "It's okay for a woman to initiate a relationship connection as long as her primary goal is to respond to the man."

I interpreted that to mean: It is appropriate for a woman to use persuasive words and actions to attract a man's interest, as long as her primary purpose is to respond to that man in an *honest manner*. In other words, she uses her charm to attract eligible men without a hidden agenda. She encourages a man to pursue her only when she has a genuine romantic interest in him.

Hot Tip

Don't approach a man because you want something from him, specifically a date, which may cause him to run to the other side of the room. Instead, extend a friendly moment of conversation to find out who he is and evaluate him as an individual.

Creative Man-Approach

I have never known a more productive way to meet a man than to ask a girlfriend to act as a go-between to break the conversational ice.

Every summer, an upscale downtown Memphis Hotel holds a rooftop soiree with appetizers, free-flowing cocktails and live music, as seventy or more guests watch the evening sun set slowly behind the river's horizon. It's a popular gathering place for Memphis singles, and my friend Janie and I thought this would be a good place to meet new men.

We had been eating, cocktailing and mingling for about an hour when I spotted a tall, sophisticated, silver-haired man standing alone at the rooftop railing. "Janie," I said, "I want you to set up an introduction with that man over there." We maneuvered our way over and we stood next to him on the pretense of wanting a better view of the river. Then, ever so subtly (not), Janie brought him into our circle of conversation by saying, "Oh my, what a beautiful sunset! By the way, my name is Janie and this is my friend Nancy." The rest is dating history.

The former mystery man and I exchanged phone numbers and arranged to meet for dinner the following Friday night. I guess I should have felt guilty about setting him up, but to my surprise he later told me, he saw me when I walked onto the rooftop and he was wondering how he could manage an introduction.

I recently read about a new dating service called "Wingman." A Wingman is a guy for hire that accompanies another man, who is less skilled at dating, to help him meet women on singles outings. The Wingman pretends to be the dating man's friend and sets him up for an introduction.

Personally, I have my own reliable source of *"Wing-Women"*: I ask a girlfriend to help me to stage a conversation with a man I want to meet. I tell her, "You have nothing to lose, I have everything to gain, and I will do the same for you."

∽ ♥ ∾

A Compliment Is the Primo Icebreaker

If you want to meet a man, smile, say something funny, make a comment about the weather, or better yet, give him a genuine compliment. A compliment is your invitation for a man to talk to you.

- "That looks like a really functional briefcase! Where did you get it?"
- "Great looking tie! I'd like to get one for my Dad's birthday. Is it new?"
- "Wow, you smell good! What is that cologne you are wearing?"
- "Your eyes are so blue! Did you get those from your Mom?"
- "Thanks for holding the door. Are there anymore at home like you?"

Camille would say, "Throw that dog a bone. Men love a compliment because they're not used to getting them." Maybe so, but it sounds to me that Camille is the one who needs to be put on a leash!

No. 3 — Tenacity Is a Man-Meeting Virtue

Man-Meeting Tenacity: Be optimistic and patient because meeting the *Love-of-One's-Life* doesn't happen over night.

Meeting new men is a numbers game. It's a throw of the dice, a draw of the card, a spin of the wheel. The more you play, the better your chances are for beating the house odds.

Without question, the hardest part of searching for the *Love-of-One's-Life* is waiting for him to make his appearance. Rather than thinking of meeting men as a neck-breaking destination, regard it as an adventurous, fun-filled journey. Consider it an opportunity to enjoy new places, meet new people and develop new friends, all of which can contribute to your self-improvement. And while you are having a good time, you may even forget that you are waiting for your Dream Man to appear.

Then—*Abracadabra!* Right before your unbelieving eyes, the *Man-of-Your-Dreams* materializes. A new man is hired into your office. A friend introduces you to a college classmate who has just moved to town. You take golf lessons and your instructor is the most patient, caring, adorable man you have ever met. Or, an eligible man is parachuting and he accidentally lands in your backyard! *Stranger things have happened.*

True Story—I met David, my soul mate, in a ladies' bathroom. Allow me to explain.

I had been divorced for nearly two years and was enjoying the fruits of my Love-All-Men dating philosophy. I had developed a social group of girl and guy friends, and I was thrilled to be dating a variety of QM. As I dated these men, I remained faithful to my promise to not get involved until I found the Man-of-My-Dreams.

It was a Friday night and, once again, I had been working out of town all week. Although I was exhausted and road-worn, I made myself get dressed and go to an event at the country club.

For an hour or so I mingled with my friends, danced, and then left to go to the ladies' room. There stood Marsha, a former co-worker of mine, primping in front of the bathroom mirror. Marsha had broken up with her boyfriend the year before and was seriously playing the dating field. Tonight she brought her most recent dating trinket—David, a recently divorced, out-of-town trial attorney who loved to wine, dine, play golf, travel, cook—you name it—David had an incredible zest for life.

In one quick moment, Marsha eyeballed me, swung around and said, "Nancy, I'm giving David to you. I'm cutting him loose tonight and you can have him!"

Shocked! Stunned! Blown Away! I could not believe what I was hearing! How could she have the nerve to say such a thing? Did she think I couldn't get my own dates? And what about poor, darling David? What gave her the right to give away another human being? Then I thought, "Why not! I was there by myself. He was cute as a button! And he came with a reference!" Recovering from her remark, I threw my head back and said, "I just might take you up on that!"

When I returned to my table, to my surprise David and Marsha were sitting right there, talking to my friends. So I sat down in the only seat available—next to him. All the while, unsuspecting David was unaware of the shaft that was headed his way from Marsha.

A short time later, as Marsha continued to ignore David, he turned to me and asked, "Would you like to dance?" I gave him my most dazzling Love-All-Men smile and purred, "Yes, I would!" We danced, laughed and talked, and when we returned to our table—Marsha had vanished.

Truly, it was a mysterious, magical meeting and over the following months, David and I fell deeply in love.

Summary

It is "creativity" that places a woman in front of the RM.
It is "optimism" and "perseverance" that help her
to wait for him.
It is her open-minded, light-hearted "approachable spirit"
that captures his attention.

Once *again*, repeat after me: "I *Love-All-Men*. I *Love-All-Men*. I *Love-All-Men*. I am going to go somewhere new, do something different and meet new men. And I am going to appreciate and have fun with the new men I meet. Until one day my very *Special Man* reveals his wonderful self to me."

Dating New Men 10

*W*hat could be more fun than meeting new men? *Why dating them, of course!*

When a woman wants to meets a man—her goal is very simple. She wants to spark his interest, get him to stop what he is doing and enjoy a moment of conversation with her. She accomplishes this by sending a subliminal message that says, *"Hi—you can talk to me."* Suddenly, his priorities change and he's wondering if she is free for dinner on Saturday night. The date is made, he picks her up, and soon she is sitting across the table from him in a candlelit restaurant. Now—what do you do on your date to have a good time and hold this man's interest?

1. The **purpose of meeting men** is to make new acquaintances or relationship connections.

2. The **purpose of dating a man** is to get to know him better while enjoying an evening of social entertainment.

3. The **reason for wanting to know more about a man** is the hope of recognizing the *Love-of-One's-Life.*

But how many times have we, as women, screwed up a date with a fabulous man because we were nervous, uncertain and felt inadequate with our dating skills? And how many times has a girlfriend called us—*upset and heartbroken*—because the wonderful man she went out with several weeks ago has never called her back? More times than we care to count.

Dating Is Supposed to Be Fun!

An Italian gourmet dinner with a delicious spumoni ending . . . watching Steven Spielberg's latest movie while sharing popcorn and holding hands . . . enjoying hot chocolates together after a brisk ski down the mountain slope. Dating should be fun, an adventure, a source of entertainment, and yet, millions of women of all ages regard dating as a grueling, nerve-racking and complicated experience. Perhaps it's partially because our mothers did not teach us how to date just *for-the-fun-of-it*. For Mom, the dating game was a *means-to-an-end* and to end her game—*she got married*.

A woman who is hard-wired to get married may find it difficult to simply relax and enjoy the dating process. For her, it is an obsessing event of trying to find a man who will whisk her away to a fairy-tale ending, and when a romantic connection doesn't happen with each new man she dates, she feels disheartened and rejected. *It's dating insanity at its finest!* Her expectations are unreasonable, unrealistic and unattainable. Will someone please tell this woman to get a grip and deal with reality—*one date at a time!*

Date like a man; take it in stride. Men assume little about the woman they are dating, the outcome of the evening, or the future of the relationship.

Just the facts, ma'am—a man only wants to deal with the cold hard facts. And the fact is, the early stages of dating for a man are little more than an opportunity to have a woman accompany him to dinner, the movies, a football game or other social function. Until a man is emotionally committed to a woman, he is able to return to his home, turn his mind off, turn his TV on, and immerse his thoughts into his job, hobbies and friends.

A Man's Invitation to Dinner is NOT an Invitation to Walk Down the Aisle.

Meanwhile, several miles away there is a hallucinating woman, fantasizing through the night of a marriage and children with a man she barely knows.

Ladies! Re-program your internal computers! Lighten up, quit being so serious and stop treating every date as if it were a life-altering event. A date is NOT an invitation to walk down the aisle. It is what it is—a *onetime* invitation for a *onetime* evening out. Think of dating as a form of entertainment, an opportunity to enjoy the company of a man and that orgasmic plate of shrimp fettuccine Alfredo that is sitting before you.

The most sensible dating advice I ever heard was from a woman named Peggy who said, "Like many of the women I know I, too, dread dating. But I know that it's something I have to do if I ever hope to find the right man for me. I have to take time to explore the possibilities and the qualities of each new man before I can intelligently write him off

Enjoy the Process of the Date While Exploring A Man's Possibilities.

as the wrong man. I know I will never regret investigating the possibility of the wrong man, but I will deeply regret not giving the right man a chance to make himself known."

Dating Tips and Tactics:

1. **Practice an *Approachable Spirit*. Practice *Loving-All-Men*.** An open-minded, relaxed attitude will demonstrate that you are friendly and easy to be with. Your accepting presence will promote an enjoyable time.

2. **Take Pleasure in Learning About a Man.** Don't be afraid to show your interest in a man by asking informative, even gently probing questions. Keep it light, however, and keep it fun. Asking questions about the things he is interested in will help the conversational flow.

   Cindy, a divorced 48-year-old hair salon owner: "I met this good-looking guy that I was dying to go out with, but he wouldn't give me the time of day. Then one night after attending a horse show I ran into him. He commented on my Roper boots and when I told him I owned horses, he immediately opened

   If You Want to Flatter a Man, Ask Him Casual Questions About Himself.

   up, telling me he was an avid horse lover, as well. We went out on a date that Saturday night. You never know what a man's hot button is!"

3. **Focus on a Man's Best Qualities and Compliment Him.** Every man is unique. Every man is special in his own way. One man has a nice smile, another is kind and considerate. Perhaps he is a connoisseur of fine art, or he has a beautiful head of hair, *or maybe not*—but

he is a very good listener. Look for his praiseworthy qualities and give him a compliment; it's the honey that keeps a man coming back for more. Be aware, however, that a man can see through insincerity more easily than he can see through glass.

A Compliment is the Honey That Keeps a Man Coming Back for More.

4. **Give Him Your Undivided Attention.** When you're talking to a man, give him your undivided attention. Stay in his moment . . . smile, look him dead in the eyes, lean into his space and make him feel as if he were the only person in the room. How flattering is it for a man to receive that kind of attention? Conversely, glancing over a man's shoulder to check out the other people in the room is the "kiss-of-death."

5. **Avoid Conversational Suicide.** Unless you want to end your date early, avoid talking about the following subjects during the early stages of dating:

   • Problems with your children, friends, family members or co-workers.

   • Complaints about dinner, the weather, your hair, or anything else.

   • Past boyfriends, husbands or other romantic relationships.

   • Bad habits, emotional hang-ups or addictions.

   • Money, sex, politics or religion.

   • Negativity about other people.

   • Future dates with him.

- Past arrest records.
- And—for heaven's sake don't talk about marriage or the biological tic-tock clock!

6. **Laugh at His Jokes. Tell Him He's Funny.** Men love to laugh at their own jokes and they love it even more when you're laughing with them. Laughing at a man's joke puts him on center stage—r*ight where he wants to be.* Laughter makes you appear attentive and engaging. It demonstrates your ability to have a good time, and it bridges the distance between two people.

7. **Tell Him That He's Smart**—*enough said!*

8. **Listen, Listen, Listen. Learn to Be a Good Listener.** No one likes to be around a "conversation hog," and men will go out of their way to avoid a woman who only wants to talk about herself. Listening to a man provides you with an opportunity to find out the things you want and need to know about him. Yes, compliment him and encourage him to talk about himself, because the more you listen, *listen, listen . . .* the more you will *learn, learn, learn.* During that conversation if a red flag pops up . . . you know what to do . . . *move'em up and head **him** out!*

9. **Communicate With Your Smile.** A sincere, friendly smile tells your date that you are enjoying his company. It also tells him that you are a confident woman.

10. **When He Calls, Let Him Know You Are Glad to Hear from Him.** There it is . . . *the telephone* . . . a man's most reliable source of communication. But what is waiting for him on the other end of the line?

    As he stares at the phone, he ponders, *"Will she be friend or foe? Will she chop my legs out from under me, or will she act like she's happy to hear from me? Good mood? Bad mood? Or maybe she already has a date for this weekend?"* It's a crap shoot for a guy because he never knows what to expect when he dials her number.

If a man takes the time and effort to call you, it is your job to offer an accepting, enthusiastic response. Your warm reception will encourage him to call back the second time, especially if you had to decline his invitation. If you are not interested in dating him be honest, yet gracious, when you decline, *"I am so flattered that you would ask me out, but I'm in the middle of giving my cat a pedicure!"* I'm joking, of course! If you're not interested in a man, temper your rejection with a dose of honesty and a side order of compassion.

11. **Try to Enjoy the Things He Enjoys.** Be open to experience the different aspects of a man's life: his friends and family, hobbies, travel and recreational interests, and food preferences. Unless it endangers your life, goes against your beliefs, or irritates your allergies, be a sport and be willing to participate in the things he enjoys—*at least once.* Then if you decide you don't enjoy Rock-A-Billy music, Sushi frog eggs or jumping out of a plane, be truthful with him and stick to those things that you can genuinely enjoy together.

12. **Be Understanding, Patient and Tolerant.** Leave the criticism, pessimism and complaints for the women who never get asked out. Try to remember that men and women think and behave differently to outside stimuli and situations. Be patient if on occasion he arrives late, if he's a bit messy, if he is sometimes distracted, withdrawn, absent-minded, or occasionally inattentive. Overlook his attempts to help you drive your car, hit a flawless golf shot, or grill a perfect

medium rare steak. I never said it would be easy to *Love-All-Men.*

13. **Ask for His Advice.** Seek a man's advice and then stand back and watch him *cock-a-doodle-do!* One of the most basic requirements for a man's happiness is that he feels needed within a relationship. At no other time does a man feel more valued than when a woman *sincerely* asks for his guidance, opinion or advice. A smart woman will listen and learn from a man's wise words and counsel, and then . . . "quietly" file away any unusable information.

14. **Ask for His Help.** In the beginning of a dating relationship it is *okay* for a woman to ask for a man's help. Choose a simple project, something that he knows how to do and that can be accomplished in a short amount of time. An easy task makes a man feel he has been helpful and has contributed to the relationship. Complicated, involved projects, however, can frustrate him and he may resent you and your request.

15. **Tell Him You Appreciate Him.** Don't forget to express your genuine appreciation for everything a man does for you, small and large. Whether it is taking you to dinner, his punctuality, his phone calls, opening your car door, listening to you talk, or his helpful advice, don't forget to tell him "thank you" for being a considerate person. Your positive feedback will let him know that he is doing the right things and he will want to be around you more often.

I had a date with a man I really liked. He wined and dined me at a marvelous restaurant, and by the end of the evening, I was certain he liked me too. But to my surprise, two weeks later, he still hadn't called back. When I told a guy friend about it, he said, "Send him a hand-written note thanking him for a wonderful evening. He'll be impressed that you took the time." So I did. He called me the day he received my note and asked me for another date. I guess sometimes it's easy to take a man for granted.

16. **Be in His Moment—Not in His Future.** Just like Superman, men have an uncanny ability to read a woman's mind when she's scripting him in as her next romantic leading man. The problem with a prematurely scripted romance is, however, if a man senses a woman's agenda, he may not stick around for the tear-jerking ending. Leave the tarot cards and Ouija board to the psychics.

17. **Have Realistic Expectations.** Or better yet, leave your expectations at home and spend the evening having a good time while getting to know your date. If a man turns out to be *Prince Charming*, well, then call yourself *"Princess"!* But, if your date fails to produce some redeeming quality—then move on. *The Ultimate Husband Hunter* is not interested in hunting male vermin. *Next!*

Stay In Control of the Date

Until a woman is certain of who a man is, she should *always* stay in control of herself and her transportation. I've said it before and I'll say it again: *be alert, be aware and be cautious!* If at anytime a woman feels uncomfortable with the man she is dating, she should not think twice about getting into her car and driving away to safety. A woman's safety is *always, always, always* the most important priority in dating.

Keeping Men as Friends

A woman can never have too many friends—*especially if they are male friends.*

Men make great friends, often times better than women. Men will share their knowledge, wisdom and advice. They will take you to nice places and entertain you. They will introduce you to their eligible male friends. If you're lucky, they will cut your trees, fix your toilet, mow your lawn and rake your leaves. And unless your male friend is gay, he won't sneak behind your back to steal your man.

A male friend can add a special quality to your life. He can help build your self-esteem by pointing out your attributes and talents; he can be a valuable source of information and offer you a different perspective on many of life's situations.

Perhaps you are a woman considering a job offer. A male friend can help you evaluate a job's hidden potential or recognize its instability. Maybe you're considering buying a house. A male friend can help you assess the structural soundness and the financial practicability of the real estate investment. Or maybe you're dating a guy that you're not quite sure of; a male friend can quickly pick up on another man's insincerity and steer you in the right direction. This is not to say that you are incapable of making your own competent, intelligent decisions. Not at all! But it sure is nice to have some male horse-sense to tap into when seeking solutions to a woman's day to day concerns.

Which brings me to the supreme reason for developing, having and keeping men as friends. The purpose of having male friends is not for a woman to have someone at her beck and call. Not on my husband hunting life! Learning to appreciate a variety of men—as friends—is the best way I know to learn how to be comfortable and confident with ALL MEN . . . which can ultimately lead a woman to her "Special Man."

Mixed Signals Do Not a Friend Make

Keeping a man as a friend, while dating him, can be a woman's biggest dating challenge. Let's face it, a man wants to date a woman to explore romantic and sexual involvement. A woman wants to date and enjoy a man without having to commit to an early sexual relationship. How then does she balance dating and friendship without fumbling the entire relationship? That's the jillion dollar man-question!

My friend Barbara, a 56-year-old divorcee, said it best, "When I start dating a man I always drive my own car to meet him and I always go Dutch treat. That way when the date is over I don't feel obligated to kiss him good-night or invite him to come into my home. It keeps a man from getting the wrong impression. Later, if I want the relationship to evolve into something else, I can always switch gears."

When a woman knows she's not interested in developing a romantic relationship with a man, she needs to get the friendship ground rules out in the open. If she continually allows a man to pick her up at the door, take her out for dinner, pick up the tabs and even accept his gifts, she is sending him a subliminal message. He will feel that he is *courting her in a romantic way* and therefore expect a physical connection as part of the relationship.

Better to Go Out With a Girlfriend Than to Selfishly Lead a Man On.

A woman who wears provocative clothing, displays salacious behavior or uses suggestive language can also s*end a man the wrong message*—unless of course, the message is that she is open to his sexual advances. Revealing clothing, inappropriate touch-ing (such as a woman's hand above a man's knee), or sexually explicit language will lead a man to think she is available to him. It is very important that a woman not portray herself as anything but a friend if she wants to be treated as such.

Confucius Says: "Woman Can't Sleep With Man Friend and Expect to Keep Man as Friend."

A true platonic relationship is a rare commodity in a single woman's universe; men are genetically hard-wired to propagate the human species and may therefore feel uncomfortable with being "only a friend."

> My friend Paul, a 34-year-old newscaster, said, "The majority of men are after one thing—SEX! And there is a 50/50 chance a man won't hang around when a woman says 'let's be friends.' To which her response should be, 'Good-night, good-bye and good riddance!'"

> My hairstylist Michael stated, "No man wants to be a friend to a woman he has slept with, because when a man sleeps with a woman, he is going to want more intimacy than a friendship can offer. Or to put it more bluntly, if he got it once, he'll want it again. And if he doesn't get it—he will resent her and drift away."

Except in rare situations, a woman is only fooling herself if she thinks she can turn a sexual relationship into a platonic one.

Out-of-Town Trips, Sex and Male Friends: Not a Winning Combination!

Trick question: What are the odds of a woman taking an out-of-town trip with a man, supposedly in the platonic sense, and a man not thinking of having sex with her? If you guessed zip, zero or zilch—you're probably right! It's tough, if not impossible, for a woman to travel with a man in the name of friendship and have that friendship remain intact. Even though most men won't admit it, when they ask a woman to go out of town with them, they are hoping that their airline points will take on new meaning. While the woman is thinking, *"I can trust myself to refrain from sex,"* the man is envisioning, *"Wine, Jacuzzi, a luxury hotel room hundreds of miles from home . . . I just might get lucky."* Tempting as it may be to accept a man's all-expense paid invitation to a sunny Pacific island, women need to think twice if they really want to keep his friendship.

Charlotte had been dating Barry for only four weeks when he popped the out-of-town question. "I've been thinking about taking a trip to Jamaica next month," Barry said, "and I would love for you to go with me. I'll take care of everything; all you have to do is show up and have a good time." Charlotte couldn't have been more surprised at Barry's offer. So far, there had been no sexual contact between them, and although she enjoyed Barry's company immensely, she still wasn't sure if he was the one for her. However, Charlotte had never been to Jamaica and thought that it would be a glorious vacation . . . but what was Barry thinking in terms of the sleeping arrangements?

A woman is only fooling herself if she believes a man is NOT thinking about sex before, during and after an out-of-town trip together.

"Barry," she began, "I have to ask you a question and please be truthful with me. If I go to Jamaica with you, are you thinking that we might have sex?" Barry weakly replied, "Why no, of course not. Well, not unless, of course—*you want to.*" Against her better judgment, Charlotte went to Jamaica with Barry and had sex with him after a night of chugalugging bucketsful of top shelf margaritas. Upon reflection, what really perplexed Charlotte about their out-of-town time together was that, while Barry was attentive and communicative at home in San Diego, he became withdrawn and tight-lipped in Jamaica. Charlotte regretted taking the trip, she regretted sleeping with Barry, and mostly she regretted that they were now unable to be friends.

The exception to this "male friend trip" theory is that there are men who are content to travel with female companions without a sexual agenda. Believe it or not, there are men who are honorable and caring and will subjugate *their* sexual desires for fear of scaring off the woman with whom they are falling in love. Lucky is the woman who knows a guy like this . . . otherwise . . . *call me when you get home to tell me how you held out!*

A Male Friend Is Worth the Exploration

A woman who adheres to the *Ultimate Husband Hunter's* philosophy does not read anything into the early stages of dating a man. She learns to take it at face value . . . merely two people going out to have a good time. She does not worry about what her date is thinking, or where the relationship is headed. She instead uses the dating process to explore the possibilities with an interesting person.

Regard a Man as Your Next Best Friend Instead of Your Next Committed Relationship.

Judith, a twice divorced 46-year-old computer program-
mer related, "My married friends set me up on a blind
date with Allen. I like Allen a lot and he likes me, too.
The problem is—I know that I could never like him in a
physical, romantic way because he smokes. I just wouldn't
feel right going out with him again because I don't want
to lead him on. What should I do?"

Judith's lack of self-confidence prevents her from developing
a friendship with a man. She is afraid to confront Allen about
his smoking because she fears she'll hurt his feelings, so instead,
her easy solution is to avoid him. Judith barely knows Allen, and
he has yet to imply a romantic interest in her, nevertheless, she
dismisses him before he has the chance to prove that he could be
a friend. Allen will, of course, be hurt by her unexplained rejection. *What kind of relationship logic is this?*

Judith should have told Allen that his cigarette smoking both-
ered her, given him a chance to refrain from smoking around her,
and then continued to see him as a friend.

She should have said to Allen, "I'm sorry, but I have a problem
with cigarette smoke and I
doubt that I could be in
a committed relationship
with a man who smokes.
It has nothing to do with
you personally, because
I think you are great guy
and I really have a good
time with you. I sincerely
hope this won't interfere
with us being friends."

*We Can't Be Mind
Readers and We Can't Be
Man-Fixers but We Can
Go Out With a Man and
Have a Great Time.*

Instead, Judith took the weak-sister way out, robbing herself—
and Allen—of a chance at friendship.

After giving it more thought, Judith said, "You're right! I do need to give Allen a chance to quit smoking when he is around me. Who knows? He could be the best male friend I've ever had."

Until a man confronts you with, "I want to be *more* than just friends," you should not assume that you are anything *but friends*. In the meantime, just be a great date and enjoy your time together. If and when the time comes that he says, *"I want more,"* and you are not so inclined, you need only smile and say, *"You're smart, you're fun, and I love being with you—but I'm not ready to be in a serious relationship."*

Words-To-Say to Keep a Man as Your Friend

Women don't know the "Words to Say" to gently discourage a man's romantic intentions, while gently encouraging his friendship. Too often a woman is too nice or too shy, and she just doesn't want to hurt a guy's feelings by telling him the most he'll ever be is a friend. Straight out of the mouths of single men are the words a woman can say to keep a man as a friend:

Roger, a single 25-year-old computer engineer says, "There's nothing that I hate more than a woman who's not honest up front about where you stand with her. Just get it out of the way and tell him you only want to be a friend. He'll figure out the rest."

Howard, a divorced 36-year-old chef states, "Let it slip out at the appropriate time that you are dating other men. A woman can discreetly get her message across by saying, 'I'd love to accept your invitation but I already have a prior engagement—thank you for thinking of me.'"

Larry, a divorced 45-year-old globe-trotting importer says, "A woman can spare my feelings by telling me, 'My life is very busy and I don't have time for a serious relationship. But I do have a good time with you and your friendship is important to me.' I, of all people, understand what it's like to have a demanding life-style."

But if you want to leave the door open for romance, listen to what Randy, a widowed 52-year-old college professor has to say: "The excuse I am willing to work with is when a woman tells me, 'I really enjoy your company but I'm very slow and cautious when it comes to committing to a serious relationship.'"

Dating and the Little White Lie

Honesty is the best policy with a man, but sometimes a harmless "little white lie" is the "social lubrication" that is needed to keep him as a friend without hurting his feelings.

I once had a date with a charming, successful banker named Matt, whose ardent hobby was duck hunting. It was during my first visit to his home when I met Molly, his 3-year-old white Labrador, whom I recognized immediately to be his intimate duck-hunting buddy. Together Matt and Molly lived happily in a small three bedroom home among duck paraphernalia, dog trophies, extensive hunting weaponry and an incalculable number of stuffed, wall-mounted ducks. The deal-breaker was, however, when Matt told me that his annual 60-day open duck-hunting season, smack in the middle of the Christmas holidays, required every minute of his time. I knew then that Matt could only be a friend.

I considered the following: Matt is a very nice man and I have a lot of fun with him. He would make a handsome escort to my social events. He could be a quality male friend. And although duck hunting is not "my thing," he is entitled to his dog and duck obsession. He just wasn't going to be a romantic connection for me. But how do I tell him I am not interested in him romantically. Do I dare tell him, "I loathe duck hunting. I hate dog hair, and your house is a duck infested disaster?" Can I possibly say this without hurting this man's feelings and keep him as a friend?

Then it came to me! Don't assume or say anything until he says or does something that implies a romantic connection. If and when he does, I will take the blame for not having time to contribute to a committed relationship. It then becomes MY problem, thereby absolving him from any wrong-doing, which could hopefully salvage the friendship. Well, the irony to this story is, I never had the chance to decline another date offer from Matt because he dumped me for another woman!

A Man May Need Time to
Think About Friendship

Be aware that telling a man that you *"just want to be friends"* can sting his ego and he may want to back away, either temporarily or permanently. If he does, give him time to reflect on his feelings, and then call him a couple of weeks later to test the water. If he then greets you with indifference or an unfriendly attitude, it may be that he is incapable of being your friend. However, if he seems receptive, invite him out for a drink or dinner—*and you pick up the tab*. Who knows, you may just gain a new male friend after all.

Words to Say

*W*e have all known women we admire, perhaps even envy, because like skillful salespeople they know exactly what to say and when to say it, to get the things they want out of life. Never is this more obvious than when they walk up to a strange man, engage him in a witty and stimulating conversation and then, as if by magic, walk away with a divine dinner invitation.

What mystical, seductive powers do these women possess that seem to capture the attention and admiration of almost every man they meet? No, it's not sorcery that they are using, rather, they have mastered the words, phrases and questions that intrigue, influence and *schmooze* with the men they meet. All women could benefit from understanding the *word power* these women have over men.

Verbal Competence in All of Life's Situations

I was 21-years-old when I discovered that there was fast cash to be made in the direct sales industry. Although I lacked the skills and knowledge of a seasoned salesperson, I possessed one strong quality—*a burning desire to succeed.* For fifteen years I worked to develop my sales skills when I realized one glaring fact: Most salespeople are *not born*—they are *made.* Successful salesmanship is a process during which they consciously and consistently:

- *Open* their conversations with the *questions* that will expose a customer's needs.
- Present convincing *words* and *statements* to describe their products and services that will fulfill those needs.
- And then . . . *close* the sale with carefully selected questions and statements that will persuade the customer to commit.

An experienced salesperson understands that proficient communication skills secure her success in life.

It didn't happen overnight, but I developed my own success-ful selling style and I later became one of the top salespeople in the cosmetics industry. I called my vocal strategy the *Words-to-Say* and the *Questions-to-Ask* in any selling situation.

How does this relate to our dating single woman? There is not a woman alive who could not benefit from having the right *Words-to-Say* and the creative *Questions-to-Ask* in every personal or business situation. Influential words, statements and questions will persuade others to *come over to your way of thinking.* It's called "selling oneself" to get what one wants out of life.

Consider the following challenging situations and the planned persuasive and influential words that can help a woman achieve her goal:

A. There's an attractive man, standing nearby at the party buffet table. What creative opening statement can a girl utter that could cause him to consider that she might pos-sibly be the most interesting woman in the room? Her *Questions-to-Ask* could be: *"Doesn't this food look incred-*

ible?" Or, *"What's the one food on this table you'd love to lock yourself in the bedroom with?"*

B. A woman is fingering through the avocados and tomatoes in the grocery store when she looks up to see a hunk standing by the lettuce bin glancing her way. What tantalizing words can she offer that would spark a conversation with him? The only reasonable produce statement is: *"Well, I have the avocado and tomato! Say, would you mind tossing me the rest of my salad?"*

C. A woman is enjoying a glass of wine at the bar of her favorite neighborhood restaurant. She is waiting to dine at a table when a professional looking man, also alone, sits two stools away and orders a beer. What clever remark can she say that will inspire a conversation between them as they wait? *"You know, the beer's really good here, but have you tried their swirling caramel apple martini?"*

Or try this one the next time you're at a bar with standing room only:

D. My friends and I are trying to get drinks, but are unable to get the attention of an extremely busy bartender. My solution: It's not what I say, but what I do that gets me what I want. I grab a straw and a white napkin off the bar, make a small surrender flag and with a big grin, I wave it to catch the bartender's eye. It has yet to offend anyone, and has always brought me a chuckle from the bartender and a quick round of drinks for me and my friends.

No, it's not voodoo or bewitching incantations that earn women the attention of the men they want to meet. It is planning, rehearsing and using influential statements and questions that encourage a man to willingly give up the last caviar canapé to the intriguing woman standing next to him at the buffet table.

Learning From My Mistakes

Knowing the right words, statements and questions can present you as an intelligent, interesting and desirable woman. It can disarm a man's resistance and set the scene for an introduction.

Whereas being unprepared, unpracticed and unskilled can cause you to fumble the perfect opportunity to meet the most intriguing man you've seen in years.

A Woman Who Is An Effective Communicator Will Also Be An Effective Person.

A woman is waiting in line to order an espresso at the coffee shop when, quite unexpectedly, *the future husband-of-her-dreams* walks up and stands beside her. *What to say? What to say?* What clever thing can she say that will break the ice, giving her a chance to meet this man without appearing clumsy or desperate? Instead, her brain turns to mush, her mouth locks up, and the *husband-of-her-dreams* walks out of her life forever before she even gets a chance to ask him how many children he wants.

Years ago I was standing in line waiting to register at the Hilton in Jackson, MS when an attractive man, with no wedding ring, walked up and stood behind me. Ridiculous as it sounds, I was smitten at the sight of this man and I really wanted to meet him. I thought, "What can I say to strike up a logical, yet enticing, conversation with this gorgeous creature?"

There he was . . . a brief breath away and I couldn't think of a single intelligent thing to say. Five minutes later, the registration clerk handed me my hotel key and I reluctantly walked away from a dinner invitation that might have hap-

pened if only I had said . . . "Hello." I blew it and I knew that I blew it because I was uncertain, ill-prepared and speechless. To this day I believe I could have shared dinner with that gorgeous man, if only I had said—WHAT?

I realized that it was a lack of self-confidence that was causing me to constantly freeze up in front of men. So, I went to work on my thoughts and I rewrote my mental scripts to reflect the humorous, charming, self-confident woman I wanted to be.

If only I had said—WHAT?

If only I had turned around and said, "I heard you mention you were from Chicago. How's the weather 800 miles away?" Or—"I've been thinking of taking a trip to Chicago this summer with my girlfriend. Could you recommend a good hotel?" Or—"Hey, how 'bout them Bears last season?" What man doesn't know how to talk about the weather, travel, food or his favorite football team?

Meeting and dating men is a continuous selling and buying process where the same situations and circumstances seem to present themselves—*over and over again.* A single woman is constantly searching, analyzing and considering which available man could be her most desirable companion or husband. A single man, on the other hand, is relentlessly shopping for a woman he considers to be "his very best deal" before committing to a serious relationship.

*"Words-to-Say" and the "Questions-to-Ask" is
a repetitive mental exercise that will sharpen your
mind, polish your language skills and help you
deliver the spontaneous, compelling words that will
encourage a man to laugh, smile and ask for your
phone number.*

Ten Tried and True Techniques for Effective, Spontaneous Communication:

1. **Be a chameleon.** Emulate the words of your skillful man-attracting girlfriends. My fearless friend Phyllis prefers to dynamite the conversational ice when she wants to meet a new man. She'll say, *"Hey, aren't you one of my ex-husbands?"* Overkill? *Maybe!* But what man can resist a woman who injects such outrageous humor into his otherwise uneventful evening?

2. **Be prepared with something interesting to say.** Familiarize yourself with the latest current events; you'll be surprised at how easy it is to interject informational tidbits into a normal conversation. Better to relate a gossip item from the *Enquirer* than to babble meaninglessly about nothing.

3. **Jazz up your reason for being out-on-the-town.** Instead of saying, *"My girlfriend and I came out to get a bite to eat,"* I'll say, *"I'm writing a dating book and my friend Dawn and*

I are looking for a man's quote for the next chapter," which really gets his attention. (You have my permission to use this one.)

4. **Prepare an interesting dialogue about who you are.** My friend Edwin calls it the "30-second elevator commercial," meaning that a person has 30-seconds to offer an interesting description of who she is before the elevator door opens and shuts. For example instead of saying *"I'm a dental hygienist,"* one might say, *"I'm an expert on smiles."* Or, rather than saying, *"I'm a bank teller,"* say, *"I'm responsible for millions of dollars every day."*

5. **Have a short, intriguing, funny story to tell.** For me, it's easy to comment on a man's cellular phone. I'll laughingly say, *"I just can't seem to hold on to my cell phone. I lost my last phone on an airplane when it fell into the toilet. Before I could stop myself, I flushed and my cell phone went flying out over the Mojave Desert."*

6. **Develop and ask light-hearted questions that require more than a yes or no answer.** Questions help to bring a person out of his shell and into your space. *"Where did you grow up? What is your all-time favorite movie? What do you like about your work?"*

7. **Tactfully prepare the personal questions you would ike to ask a man.** If you want to get a peek at his history, family or financial situation, ask, *"Do you have school-age children?"* Don't ask, *"Does your ex-wife ever have to hunt you down for her child support?"* If you want to know whether he has any addictions, ask, *"I'm going to pick up a bottle of wine before you come over Friday night. Will one bottle be enough?"* Not, *"Have you ever been committed for a drinking problem?"*

8. **Know what to say at the end of a date.** The ending of a first date can be as awkward for a man as it is for a woman. If you like him, but think he might need a little reassurance, you can say, *"I had a great time; we'll have to do this again."* But if you're not interested in seeing him again, something short and sweet will do. *"Thanks for a lovely evening,"* with a handshake may be sufficient to discourage him from calling you again. Knowing what to say at the end of date can save you from tripping on your tongue and giving him the wrong message.

For some, the *Words-to-Say* and the *Questions-to-Ask* may sound like an elementary activity, but it is an exercise that can help you to be a precise, effective, influential communicator in every area of your life. After all, if one can't learn from a verbal mistake—*what good is the mistake?*

Be a Giver—Not a Taker

A pretty smile, an outgoing personality, a real way with words—*it doesn't mean a thing* if she is a selfish, self-serving woman. For Camille, it was all about her. It was about getting what she wanted, when she wanted it . . . and if she didn't get what she wanted, she would throw a screaming hissy fit. Even with all of Camille's charm and cuteness, when the men in her life realized that she was a *Taker*, they would pack their bags and flee.

Camille was looking for her fourth husband when she set her sites on Paul, a 49-year-old real estate developer. She said, "I knew I had to keep up the appearance of a considerate and caring person to get Paul to propose, so occasionally I would treat him to lunch or a movie." One year later Paul and Camille said "I do." Two years later she was screaming at him for throwing *his* money away on golf (his only hobby). Six years later Paul was asking Camille for a divorce. No matter how dazzling a woman is, a man will eventually resent a *Taker*.

Dating is a Reciprocal Process

A *Taker* is always concerned with *what's in it for her.* Who is going to buy her dinner? Who is going to lavish her with pretty things? Who is going to be responsible for her happiness? She takes and takes and takes, until all that is left is a man's distrust, disrespect and disfavor.

Some Women Are Calculators and Some Women are Manipulators— Don't be Either!

A woman who allows a man to shoulder all the dating responsibilities will eventually sacrifice her appeal and influence within the relationship.

By contrast, a gracious *Giver* is considerate of the men she meets and dates. She takes responsibility for her own happiness, as well as contributes to the happiness of others. Her motivation for giving is simply to make another person feel good. The amount of her giving is not as important as

Being a Giver and Not a Taker is an Investment in Finding the Right Man.

the fact that she gives what she can, she gives when it's appropriate, and she gives with no strings attached.

A woman without a dating agenda is empowered to shape her own destiny.

Men Respect *Givers*—Not *Takers* and They Recognize the Difference

John, a single 27-year-old architect engineer says, "In the beginning Ellie appeared to be fun, flexible and open-minded. Only weeks into dating her, however, I noticed she seemed to be more interested in the dollars I spent on entertaining her than the quality of our time spent together. I guess the tip-off was when she couldn't hide her irritation with me when I asked her to go camping at a trout fishing resort. *"You mean in the sticks?!?!"* she shrieked. That's when I decided she was a high maintenance girl and in my book high maintenance is rarely an attractive quality."

Thomas, a 50-year-old corporate executive comments, "You want to know what really impresses a man—*reach for the check!* Not like you don't really mean it, but seriously, generously pick up the tab. Wow! Now that's power!"

Small Gestures of Appreciation Will Earn a Man's Respect

It's the little things that count. Sometimes it's the creative or the unexpected that will win a man's appreciation. For example:

- Surprise him with a bottle of wine and an appetizer when he comes to pick you up for a date.
- Take a live potted flower to his house; every time he waters it he will think of you.
- Use your lipstick to draw lips and a cute message on his bathroom mirror before leaving his home.
- Pick up a sweet treat or his favorite magazine at the grocery checkout.
- Send him a thank-you note after a wonderful evening.
- Extend an unexpected lunch or movie invitation.
- Bake him a birthday cake.
- Cook him a simple dinner.
- Burn a CD of your favorite music to play in his car when you go on a date and give it to him as a gift at the end of the evening.

Do something nice for a man and watch him court you as if you were the special flavor of the month. Or let a man do all the dating work, and watch him go down the street to shop at another ice cream parlor.

Personal Ten Commandments

I knew it was time to change my life and the way I approached men. I wanted them to be attracted to me and take me out on dates. More importantly, I wanted the *Right Man* to pursue me for a serious, committed relationship. To do that, I would have to change a lifetime of established negative attitudes and behavior; it seemed an insurmountable task.

Easier said than done! *Stinkin-thinkin* had become a way of life for me. I needed to re-train my brain, re-program my negative thoughts and curb the caustic remarks that seemed to fly out of my mouth.

I went to work on my negative side, but soon discovered that my good intentions were not enough. How quickly I slipped into my old ways! I would make a snide remark about my ex-husband; I was impatient with a waiter, or I talked too much about myself. I needed

A woman who thinks she doesn't need to change— probably needs change more than she realizes.

something to keep me on track. I needed a *moment-to-moment* reminder of the qualities of the accepting, considerate, tolerant and fun-loving woman I wanted to be.

I Began to Write My "Personal Ten Commandments"

Commandment No. 1: *My self-worth comes from my internal self.* I am fully pleasing to me and I should not look to another person for approval. I celebrate my individuality and who I am. I like myself.

Commandment No. 2: *Honor and listen to my intuition.* Be true to myself. If I allow my intuition to guide me, I will learn to make good decisions.

Commandment No. 3: *Love-All-Men.* Respect, value and appreciate all men. Better yet, respect, value and appreciate myself, as well as all people.

Commandment No. 4: *Develop my Approachable Spirit.* An open-minded, welcoming presence will inspire everyone to seek out my company.

Commandment No. 5: *Be a Giver—Not a Taker.* Giving without an agenda contributes to my personal power and helps people to realize that I am genuine.

Commandment No. 6: *Live in the moment, wherever I am.* Learn to appreciate and be content with whatever I am doing.

Commandment No. 7: *Never talk about anyone in a negative way*—especially the men in my past.

Commandment No. 8: *Limit cocktails.* Drinking can distort my ability to reason, as well as harm my feminine mystique, possibly ruining an opportunity to date a *QM*.

Commandment No. 9: *Be a good listener.* Don't interrupt. If I am doing all the talking, I am not learning about the person in front of me.

Commandment No. 10: *Quit trying so hard.* If I have done my absolute best, then my best should be good enough.

After I wrote my *Personal 10 Commandments* I laminated two purse-size copies, one for my desk and one for my wallet, as a constant reminder of what I was trying to accomplish. I read my words of encouragement before leaving the house for a date, and then re-read it again privately during the evening, to keep me at my very best.

> *The Personal 10 Commandments Was My Written Commitment to a Better Life.*

Today, whenever I glance at the *Personal 10 Commandments*, I realize how easy it is to fall back into the old negative patterns. They remind me that there is always room for personal growth.

Code of Ethics

*K*nowledge is power and a woman must control her power.

A woman who has self-confidence realizes that her feminine persuasive style can have a strong influence over a man's feelings and actions. It is this kind of power that gives a woman the intrinsic responsibility of honoring the emotions and integrity of men. This is the *Ultimate Husband Hunter's* "Code of Ethics."

A self-confident woman understands that she has control over her feelings, thoughts and the events in her life. She also realizes that she has the capacity to inspire a man's interest in her. It is important that we remember to treat all the men we meet and date in a sincere, honest and respectful manner, while we search for our special man.

> *Self-confidence with men . . . it was something I hungered for all my life. I condemned and discounted Camille's manipulating ways, and yet, I was fascinated by her ability to attract men. She once said to me, "I can have any man that I want if I set my mind to it." And indeed she could. So I took her*

man-attracting tactics, refined them and combined them with my sensitivity and sincerity. It was a dating strategy, so monumental and so effective that it required its own code.

Principles of the Code:

Principle No. 1—*Do not lead a man on.* Do not say or do anything that could be interpreted or give him the impression that you are open to a romantic or sexual relationship, when in truth—you're not.

Principle No. 2—*Do not use a man for selfish gain.* Don't take advantage of his generous nature by accepting dinner invitations, gifts, or help with household repairs in the "name of romance" if you don't share his feelings.

Principle No. 3—Do not disrespect men. *In all ways, respect the men you meet and date,* because you want the same respect in turn.

Do not use your knowledge and charm to hunt or trap a man in whom you are not interested.

Part Three

The Saboteurs

"If only there were a magic mirror in which we could see
ourselves as others see us."
—Nancy Nichols

Saboteurs of the "Love-All-Men" Spirit

I ask you: What sane, single woman would purposely block the advances of an eligible, attractive QM? What woman—in her right mind—would mindfully display the type of behavior that is known to run men off? What intelligent woman would do such a counterproductive, hideous thing? The *Saboteurs* of the *"Love-All-Men" Spirit*—that's who!

I asked myself these questions hundreds of times . . . and I am willing to bet that you have asked yourself these questions as well:

- Am I sabotaging my chances of meeting and dating good men?
- Am I displaying the attitudes and behavior that turn men off?
- Am I running off a QM who could have otherwise been interested in me?
- Ask yourself, *"Are you?"*

Saboteurs of the *Love-All-Men Spirit* are women who display negative, critical attitudes, self-serving dispositions, or guarded and mistrusting natures. Men who may have wanted to date them *didn't* because of the woman's negative disposition. And men who dated them—*stopped!* What are these women doing that habitually sabotages the early stages of their relationships with men? And do these women not see what they are doing?

One of the most difficult things to do in life is to see our-selves as others see us.

I always considered myself to be a pretty good catch, but my erratic relationship history gave me cause to stop and think, "Is it possible that I see myself as one type of person . . . and yet, outwardly portray myself as someone entirely different?" Then I realized the ugly truth. Instead of the accepting, caring, easy-going person I envisioned myself as being, I was *unknowingly* projecting just the opposite to those who crossed my path.

Ironically, I displayed the very same negative attitudes and behavior that I condemned in many of the women I knew. I was anxious and needy. I was critical, scrutinizing and judgmen-tal. My fears and mistrust made me appear aloof, unfriendly and unavailable to men. Indeed, it was a humbling day when I real-ized that men were not interested in me because of my outward negative demeanor.

It was painful to admit my own character flaws and weak-nesses—*but I finally did.* With my private humiliation behind me, I pledged to replace my bad attitudes and beliefs with a new accepting, affirming and approving mindset.

It is my firm belief that one of the underlying reasons that so many women have relationship problems is quite simply that *they are unaware of their negative attitudes and counterproductive behavior.* They do not recognize that what they are saying and doing is sabotaging their efforts. They cannot see themselves *as others see them.* A woman who projects negativity and mistrust is only hurting herself and her chances of being with a QM.

Perhaps every woman needs to ask herself:

- Am I unknowingly projecting a negative attitude toward the men I meet?

- Is a negative attitude causing me to appear aloof and unfriendly?

- Could it really be true that I am the one who is responsible for my relationship problems?

17

Saboteur No. 1:

"I'm Fearful. I'm Mistrusting. I'm Cautious About Getting Involved With Men."

eet Saboteur No. 1. She's afraid of emotional intimacy, of loving a man deeply because he may exploit, abuse or betray her. She's afraid to let a man get too close because he may disapprove, condemn or reject her.

Saboteur No. 1 keeps men safely at an arm's length because she is afraid of being hurt. Someone, at sometime, taught her to fear and mistrust men. She erects an invisible, impenetrable wall to protect her fragile emotions. Impenetrable, because the walls she has built are held together by a mortar of fear, resentment and anger from her past relationships.

Sandra, a 27-year-old registered nurse tells her story: "Daniel was my first and only love in high school. I willingly gave my love, loyalty and virginity to him because I trusted him and believed his pledge of marriage and a secure future together. College changed everything."

After two years of a committed relationship, Daniel and Sandra graduated from high school and attended different colleges, separating them by 300 miles. For the next two years they telephoned one another daily and saw each other frequently on weekends. From every indication, their relationship seemed solid and on track. Then, in her sophomore year, a week before Christmas break, Sandra's world was shattered. Daniel telephoned her to say that he would not be coming home for Christmas because he was now engaged to a girl he had meet during his freshman year. Sandra had been betrayed.

Sandra had trusted Daniel. She believed that he was faithful to her while they were apart, and she believed that after graduation he wanted to marry, have children and start a wonderful life together. *Why wouldn't she feel betrayed?* At the end of every phone conversation, he expressed his love and loyalty to her, and every weekend that they were together, they had passionate, intimate sex.

Saboteur No. 1: She's Hyper-Sensitive to the Criticisms and Opinions of Others.

Everything that Daniel said and did had led Sandra to believe nothing had changed, when in reality it was all a façade. Sadly, Sandra never recovered from Daniel's betrayal.

∾ ♥ ∾

Lindsey, a 42-year-old divorcee, relates her hurtful past: "Robert and I married right out of college. During our first year of marriage I became pregnant, followed by a second pregnancy a year and a half later.

I had an exciting commercial interior design career planned, but Robert and I agreed, I would be a stay-at-home mom until our sons graduated from high school. Thirty years later, Robert abruptly left me for a 29-year-old female executive in his office. He betrayed me; he was unfaithful to me and he deserted me."

Robert's betrayal almost destroyed Lindsey. She had dedicated her entire life to him and the boys. And now her sons were grown and married with children of their own. Robert had a new young bride and there she was in her mid-fifties, alone and struggling to start a new career, while confronting the challenges of a single woman's social life. All the while, Lindsey desperately tried to numb the pain, anger and bitterness she continued to feel toward her ex-husband for his deception, infidelity and his abandonment of her for a younger woman.

Janice, a 51-year-old, was a three-time divorcee with a history of relationship causalities. Her needy, controlling behavior and critical fault-finding continually serve to destroy her relationships. Janice relates her story:

"I grew up in a home where I witnessed my father abuse and mistreat my mother. I was the oldest of three siblings and I too reaped the wrath of his critical, condemning anger. At age eighteen, I married to get away from home."

Janice had been emotionally abused by her father. As an adolescent, he scolded her unjustly causing her feelings of worthlessness; as a teen his derogatory comments about her faddish clothing demeaned her developing sexuality.

The result was that she learned destructive relationship skills from her parents and she later used these skills in her adult relationships. She learned to criticize, manipulate and blame others. She learned to fear and mistrust men just like she mistrusted her father. It's no surprise that now she has a problem meeting men, dating them and maintaining a relationship with them.

Saboteur No. 1 Hides Herself Behind A Wall of Fear and Mistrust.

These three women were betrayed, mistreated or abused by a loved one in their past. They are now self-protective and guarded. While as children they were trusting and loving by nature, their fear and mistrust as adults prevent them from being affectionate and authentic. They project a reserved and unapproachable presence causing potential suitors to back away from them. Men who become involved with them struggled with their issues, eventually lost heart and drifted away; it took too much work to maintain a relationship with these damaged women.

Saboteur No. 1 locks herself inside an isolating, protective prison with the very fears and emotional pain she so desperately seeks to escape.

18

Saboteur No. 2:

"I'm Picky. I'm Choosy. I'm Discriminating About the Men I Date."

We live in a society that warns women to be discriminating about the men with whom they associate. Be picky. Be choosy. Be careful. One internet dating service calls it a woman's "must haves" and "can't stands." Do your mental checklist and if he doesn't measure up—*don't waste your time.*

Granted, a woman should adhere to her "must haves" and "can't stands"; she should establish standards for choosing a man with healthy dating behavior. A woman needs to know *what is acceptable* to her in a man, as well as what is unacceptable in the man she befriends, dates and one day plans to marry. BUT—when a woman is too picky, choosy and discriminating—*it can backfire,* for she is apt to project an unapproachable presence to the men she wants to attract.

❧ ♥ ❧

I am ashamed to admit that there was a time in my life when I thought I was too good to associate with many types of men. Like Camille's sister Kitty, my automatic knee-jerk reaction was also to reject the squatty, little bald man in the frightful red plaid shirt for even a moment of casual conversation because I was too busy scoping out the room for, *what I considered to be*, a more suitable man.

Truth can be an unpleasant serum to swallow.

I thought of myself as a first-string eligible woman, when in truth, I was the "Queen of Scrutiny." I was a hyper-perfecting, fault-finding woman whose low self-esteem left little room for the shortcomings of others.

I have always heard that insecure, abusive people will belittle, criticize and beat down another so that they can build themselves up. It's called an inferiority complex. They try to act bigger and better than others to overcompensate for their insecurities and low self-esteem issues.

My personal affliction was perfectionism. I wanted to believe that I was a desirable, fascinating, intelligent, even sexy, woman. I wanted to think that any man would be lucky to have me. Inside, however, I secretly felt flawed and self-conscious in a man's presence. To compensate, I demanded perfection in myself, as well as the men I dated. My resulting over-inflated ego, and the unreasonable standards I set for myself, made it easy for me to believe that others were flawed and unworthy of my time. *Nothing could have been further from the truth!*

Yes, I was overly critical about the men with whom I associated. I discovered, however, that men were created for a variety of praiseworthy reasons. Men offer friendship; they provide valuable knowledge, information and wisdom; they willingly help with tedious, laborious and difficult chores. Men support a woman's efforts and help build her self-esteem and confidence. They can be a rock of emotional support during a personal crisis. And *Lo! and Behold!* these men come in a surprising variety of packages.

Fortunately I am now willing to give a man a chance to show me his best qualities and enjoy a moment of his company. *But please understand*—there are many men to whom I will never, ever be physically or romantically attracted. Understand also, that there are many men who, because of their bad behavior or nasty attitudes, will never get a moment of my time or attention. However, my *Love-All-Men Philosophy* tells me to appreciate and value a wider range of men in a wider range of circumstances.

Saboteur No. 2: Her Fault-Finding, Hyper-Perfectionism Destroys Her Feminine Nature, Along With a Man's Interest.

No man is ever good enough for Saboteur No. 2. Nor can he measure up to her unattainable standards. No man is interested in confronting her pretentious, unapproachable presence.

Yes, a woman should be choosy about the men she dates; *the problem is* . . . when she's *too* choosy she forfeits the opportunity to make new male friends, meet new people, and all the social events that go with it. She, instead, spends her dateless nights at home with a lonely Cosmopolitan, a bowl of cheese dip and a bag of chocolate kisses, while watching *Sex In The City* reruns of Carrie, Miranda, Samantha and Charlotte having all the dates, all the fun and all the real kisses.

19

Saboteur No. 3:

"I'm Critical. I'm Opinionated. I Run Men Off."

*T*he deadliest of the Saboteurs is the woman who, with her fault-finding, scornful mindset, typically looks for the worst in men. She dispenses regular doses of critical advice and strong opinions. She sows negativity and dissension; she reaps indifference, contempt and rejection. New men are afraid to meet her because they are leery of her inapproachability. Those who know her, avoid her because they are aware that she is controlling, manipulating, disapproving and rejecting. Men instinctively turn away from her because they sense her negativity.

Saboteur No. 3 Disfigures Her Feminine Beauty With a Disapproving, Hypercritical Mindset.

Many times, the woman who is most eager to point out a man's flaws and imperfections is *the very* woman who is unwilling to recognize and admit to her own faults. Veronica was such a woman.

I met Veronica, a divorced retired flight attendant through a single's social organization and then again at church. She had a history of divorces and failed relationships; she complained incessantly about the men in her life. She ran men off with her negativity and constant criticism. When a man dumped her she blamed the breakup on *his* shortcomings.

I once invited Veronica to a casual gathering at my home with a group of friends. I was dumbstruck when she asked me to exclude Bob, my newest male friend, from the guest list. "There's something about him I just don't like," Veronica said to me. Ignoring her advice and request, I invited Bob to my party. As a result, I had several wonderful dates with this fascinating man. Later, Veronica admitted to me that she had Bob mixed up with another man she met only briefly in the recent past. No surprise here, because Veronica had a shortsighted, hypercritical opinion of most of the men she met.

Men will continue to run from Veronica like their pants are on fire, and she will continue to scratch her head in bewilderment, wondering *what went wrong with her latest, greatest relationship?* Veronica's negative, critical mindset is a lethal, double-edged sword that repeatedly cuts off her nose to spite her very own face.

Saboteurs of the *Love-All-Men Spirit* are the women who habitually sabotage their chances of ever meeting, dating and being with a wonderful man.

They snub a man for his clothing choices, physical appearance and interests. They slight him for his occupation, social status and background. They prejudge, criticize and disqualify a man before he even has a chance to reveal his best and enduring qualities.

What man is able to endure Saboteur's No. 3's frosty, condemning presence?

Part Four

The "Well-Equipped Woman"

*"The first step to significant personal improvement
is one's willingness to be totally honest about
those things that need improving."*
—Nancy Nichols

Intro: Gearing Up

*T*he *Ultimate Husband Hunter's* mission in life is simple. She strives to be the best she can be in order to attract the attention and interest of qualified eligible men. Once she has done her personal work, her goal is to meet and "capture" a *QM* who is worthy of her love, affection and loyalty . . . someone she can proudly refer to as the *Love-of-Her-Life*.

Life, dating and relationships are an ongoing, learning processes. To be the best that one can be, one must seek the sage advice of professional counselors and wise friends, develop one's spirituality, study self-help and self-improvement books, and observe and glean information from one's skillful female friends. Most importantly, one must realize that it is one's past experiences which provide one with life's most valuable lessons.

Our safari continues as the *Ultimate Husband Hunter* equips herself with the characteristics, qualities and expertise that are known to attract *QM*.

Discovering 21 *Self-Confidence*

*Self-Confidence is a woman's most alluring
and important asset.*

There is nothing—I *mean nothing*, which attracts a man to a woman more than a healthy level of self-confidence. It intrigues him. It allures him. He can't resist it. A man will give up his front row seats to the Super Bowl, pass up an Alaska fishing trip, and will even relinquish the custody of his TV remote control, just to be in the presence of a self-confident woman.

If only she could walk up to a retail counter to purchase a lifetime supply of self-confidence! Regrettably, life is not so simple.

Confidence is freedom from doubt; it is the belief in one's judgment, abilities and power. It inspires us to be the best we can be, and go after the things that are important to us.

Self-esteem is the favorable regard for oneself; it is the quality of feeling worthy of respect. It is the opinion that one has of one's self, based on a perceived image, values and position in life. **Low self-esteem**, on the other hand, is poor self-image, causing one to feel unworthy of respect, love, and a quality life.

Tragically, if a woman does not develop a healthy level of self-confidence as a child or adolescent, she may suffer from low self-esteem later in life. Low self-esteem causes her to doubt her own abilities and to make bad choices. It can hinder her in the workplace, create difficulties with her family and friends, and prompt her to participate in dysfunctional relationships that will further erode her self-worth.

Love-All-Men Promotes Self-Confidence

"Self-consciousness is the No. 1 enemy of self-confidence," states More-selfesteem.com. I couldn't agree more. At one time or another, every woman has felt out-of-place, insecure on a date, or self-conscious when walking into a roomful of people. Authorities theorize that self-confidence is a learned quality, and that anyone can have it. Again, I wholeheartedly agree. The question is, if one does not have it, where and how does one achieve this seemingly elusive quality?

Some experts say that confidence can be acquired through positive personal assertions, such as:

- Quit trying to please others, learn to please yourself.
- Face your fears, forget your failures.
- Think positive thoughts, speak and act as though you were confident, even if you're not.
- Acknowledge your small accomplishments.
- Pamper yourself, eat healthy and exercise.
- Set priorities and achievable goals.

In other words, brainwash yourself until you truly are self-confident. *Good advice*, but it doesn't always work and it doesn't always stick.

More-selfesteem.com offers their confidence building approach: *"Learn how to keep your attention off yourself . . . If you feel self-conscious in a social situation, it's usually because you don't have enough to do! Focus on what your purpose in the situation is. Whether you're there to: find out if you like the other people in the situation; make others feel comfortable; find out some information; (or) make business contacts."* Now that sounds like a plan.

The key to self-confidence is to take the focus off yourself.
You will soon forget that you had low self-esteem.

If ever there were a crash course on how to be a self-confident woman—*this is it!*

In any situation, *take the focus off of yourself,* step out of the comfort zone you are accustomed to and investigate and appreciate a wider range of men. The more men you meet, and consequently appreciate, the more men you will attract. The more men you attract, the more confident you will become. The

Self-Confidence Insight

A self-confident woman believes she is worthy of a man's pursuit, which consequently, gets his attention. On the other hand, a woman who overtly chases a man may undermine her confidence when she doesn't get his interest.

new attention you receive from these men could be *the very thing you need* to boost your self-esteem. My experience is that when I validate and appreciate men, they will in turn validate and appreciate me, which in the past jump-started my belief that I was, *indeed*, a unique and valuable person.

Modesty and Self-Confidence Go Hand-In-Hand.

A woman is most beautiful when she is seemingly unaware that she is beautiful. She is most sexy when she doesn't realize that she is sexy. She is most alluring when her confidence is seasoned with a dash of modesty.

> *A male friend once told me, "You are so hot!" When I blushed and protested, he said, "That's what makes you so sexy. You don't know that you are!"*

Conversely—being overconfident and playing "hard-to-get" can be a big turn-off.

> Don: "Men enjoy being with a woman who is comfortable with herself, because she is easy to be with. But when a woman is overconfident, she may come off as cocky and insincere and will reap his rejection and disdain."

The Elements of a Self-Confident Woman

- Be cheerful, charming, and flirtatious—*yet* honest, sincere and caring.
- Be unbiased, *but* selective about the men you meet and date.

- Be respectful of his time and personal space, and be considerate and mindful of your needs as well.
- Be a courteous giver and a gracious receiver.
- Be unafraid to initiate a social invitation, phone conversation or relationship connection.
- Offer your guy small gestures of attention without fear that he will reject or misread your intentions: i.e., briefly grasping his hand, walking arm in arm or giving him a considerate hug.
- Be mindful of maintaining an attractive personal appearance.
- Trust your intuition. I repeat, *trust your intuition!*

The guidelines in this chapter are a beginning to self-confidence. It can take years of reading, counseling and self-affirmations to undo the low self-esteem issues that have taken years, maybe even decades, to develop. I strongly recommend that you read books on the topic and receive counseling from qualified professionals. In the meantime, the advice in my book could be an excellent starting point for increasing your self-confidence . . . or it could be an enhancement to the self-improvement work that you have already begun. Either way, the quest for self-respect, self-esteem and self-confidence have to start somewhere. Why not start with the relationship philosophy in my book?

Honoring Your Intuition

22

Intuition is a woman's most valuable resource.

A woman, who listens to, honors and follows the direction of her **Intuition—her gut feelings**—is a woman who trusts herself. Each time she follows her own judgment and values her abilities, she enriches her sense of self-worth. A self-trusting woman is more able to discipline her emotions, thoughts and actions; she leans on her instincts, abilities and a positive attitude to give her courage to go after all that she wants in life.

The "Sixth Sense"

So powerful is our Intuition that it is called the "Sixth Sense."

Every woman is born with the gift of Intuition. It is the best friend she will ever have in her life, for it exists solely to protect, guide and influence her to make decisions that are in *her* best interest.

Intuition gives us insight into the things that happen in our lives. It is a deeper sense of understanding and discernment regarding difficult problems that seem to have no easy solution. It is the capacity to access the true nature of a situation, and to understand better the motives and reasons behind a person's actions.

Typically, Bad Decisions Do Not Come From Your Intuition

Incredibly, Intuition is the innate understanding and foresight into those things *that have not yet happened!* It is the ability to grasp the hidden nature of people and the unknown outcome of a situation.

A Woman Without Intuition Is Like A Plane Without Radar

She flies blindly at night, with no direction, oblivious to the danger that lies ahead. It is not until she collides with the consequences of her bad decision that she realizes the foolishness of her choice. By then it's too late, her folly is done, and she's left wondering . . . *"What could I have done differently?"*

A woman who continually ignores, compromises and rebuffs her intuition will end up with a weak sense of judgment. She will struggle to understand the problem people and the difficult situations that come into her life. She will not trust her assessment of men and will consequently make bad relationship decisions. She won't understand *why* she keeps winding up with the *Wrong Man.*

∽ ♥ ∾

Susanna, a 29-year-old single dance instructor relates: "After only a few dates with Jack, something in my gut told me not to get involved with him. Right from the start he tried too hard to be Mr. Nice Guy, with all of his compliments, gifts and suggestions of a future together. I even got a preview of his cynical side one night, when he snapped at our waitress for her clumsy service. Sure enough, when Jack knew that he had me, he began belittling me with the same biting, fault-finding criticisms.

The problem with Jack was that he suffered from low self-esteem; to build himself up, he demeaned and criticized those closest to him. At first I withstood his spiteful remarks, and when that didn't work, I threatened to leave him. But somehow he always managed to twist the truth to justify his bad behavior.

From the very beginning something inside me screamed, "Get out." But I discounted my instincts and forged ahead with a relationship that was fated to hurt me. It took less than a year for Jack's abusive nature to ravage my hope and happiness.

I finally disconnected with this awful man and I am still trying to recover from his emotional battering. If only I had listened to the small warning voice inside me that tried to save me at the beginning of the relationship."

Susanna's *Intuition* tried desperately to warn her that the man she was dating, and the kind of relationship he was offering, was predestined to be a *big mistake*. But she couldn't stand the thought of being alone, so she waged war against her *Intuition*, abandoned her common sense, and recklessly entered a relationship with the *Wrong Man*. If she continues to compromise and ignore her *Intuition*, she will eventually succeed in suppressing that part of her spiritually.

The silencing of one's Intuition is a severe loss of the insight and wisdom that one needs to make good choices in life.

Games That Undermine Intuition

The Blame Game

He says or does something that is deceitful, hurtful or demeaning, and then in an effort to avoid responsibility for his harmful behavior, blames you for the ensuing conflict. His behavior is questionable and all the evidence points to a dysfunctional personality, but because he is extremely convincing, you begin to doubt yourself. Nevertheless, a small voice of concern inside you cries out, *"Don't allow that kind of behavior. You don't deserve to be treated that way."*

Somewhere, just below our consciousness, is our intuitive voice pleading to be heard. You know the truth. Logically, you know he's lying, and you know he's shifting the blame to conceal his own bad behavior. But you don't want to give him up, so you tune out your knowing voice, disregard the truth, reject your need for self-preservation . . . and stay in a toxic relationship.

It is a woman's foolish and reckless decisions that can do the most damage to her self-confidence and self-esteem.

∾ ♥ ℮

The Put-Down Game

When I was growing up I heard the words, "You shouldn't feel that way. You're being overly sensitive." Later as an adult, I was told, "You heard that wrong; that's not at all what I said or meant." If this were true . . . then *why* did I feel so *bad* inside? And why did I feel hurt and mistreated? Because my gut instinct recognized the truth—*even when I didn't!*

The constant put-down remarks of others can eventually teach a woman to mistrust her feelings and doubt her judgment.

For the better part of my life I was afraid to make decisions. I didn't trust my judgment in the business world; I was uncertain of how to handle relationship difficulties with a girlfriend or a co-worker; I felt inadequate in parenting my children. And when it came to *MEN!* . . . I was constantly on the doorstep of a girlfriend, tearfully seeking her advice on *what to do!* I felt weak, confused and ineffective because the only thing I knew to believe—*was what others told me to believe.*

For two decades I played the role of a victim. *ENOUGH!* Give me back my life! Methodically, I began to access the issues in my life. I began to look earnestly for the truth in each problem, the authenticity of each person, and the accuracy of each difficult situation. Consciously, I listened for advice from my intuitive voice. Once I felt I heard the truth, I trusted my

When your Intuition is a faint whisper, you must accept on faith that it will make decisions that are in your best interest.

instincts and executed what I considered to be the best solution for each problem, person or situation. At first, trusting myself was perplexing and awkward, an agonizing process, but I discovered that the more I relied on my *Intuition*, the stronger became my intuitive vibes and the more accurate became my decisions.

True personal power comes when a woman can depend on herself to make the important decisions in her life.

How's Your Intuition?

1. Do you have a history of dating and committing to men who demonstrate harmful relationship behavior?

2. Do you seek constant relationship advice or approval from one or more of your girlfriends, because you can't seem to trust your own judgment about a man?

3. Do you disregard solicited advice from a girlfriend to stop dating a man with bad behavior?

4. Do you sometimes secretly question a man's motives and attitudes, but keep dating him anyway?

If you answered *yes* to any of these questions, my next question is . . . *why* is it so hard for you to walk away from the obvious unkind behavior of a dysfunctional man?

Intuition is like a muscle. The more you use it, the stronger it gets. The more you pay attention to it, the *wiser* becomes the counsel, the more *significant* becomes the advice, and the more *audible* becomes the message.

Listen to your Intuition and you will find your own wisdom, which will guide you toward a loving, healthy relationship.

Smile

A woman's smile is her most effective and influential resource.

There is one piece of ammunition that a woman should value more than any other. It is her *Smile.*

A smile is the heart, soul and embodiment of a woman's charm, and charm can be a husband hunter's lethal weapon—*in a very good way, of course.* It is what attracts a man to a woman and makes him give up, give in and fall in love.

A Woman's Most Important Body Language Is Above Her Neck

Body language statistics say:

- Up to 93% of all communication is non-verbal.
- 60% of getting a positive message across is by way of body language.
- We have 10 to 30 seconds to make a favorable first impression.

Friendly, expressive people are attractive people. Although the eyes are the mirror of the soul and the most expressive part of the human body, it is a woman's warm and inviting smile that is the universal non-verbal language which projects friendliness and approachability.

Paul and Phyllis

A woman's smile is a powerful flirting tool that lets a man know that she finds him interesting.

Paul, a 47-year-old divorced architect, "After a hard day at work, I stopped at Arnie's Bar for a quick beer before going home. There she was, standing by a table with a group of girlfriends, the most intriguing woman I'd seen in a long time. I wanted to meet her, and my guess was, she wouldn't mind meeting a nice guy. If only she would look in my direction, I thought. And then she turned, saw me staring at her, and flashed me a beautiful smile. *Wham!* The next thing I knew I was across the room, standing in front of her."

Phyllis' side of the story: "I met my girlfriends for a birthday party at a neighborhood club when I saw Paul walk through the door. I told my girlfriends, 'You see that guy over there? I'm probably going to marry him.'

I recently read an article on 'how-to flirt' in a magazine and when I saw Paul, I decided to try it out. I waited for him to look in my direction, and when he did, I made eye contact, nodded and smiled. Within minutes I felt Paul's hand on my shoulder and he asked me if he could buy me a drink. We dated for three years until we finally married."

David and Nancy

A woman's friendly, flirtatious smile is more physically attracting than any other sexual gesture. It is more inviting than a provocative stare, deep cleavage, pouty lips or long, lanky legs.

David, "The first thing I noticed about Nancy was her big beautiful smile. It was a grin that told me she was enthusiastic, spontaneous and open. I told myself, 'This woman would be fun to be with,' so I asked her to dance."

Nancy, "I have always been told that I have a great smile; eventually I realized that it was one of my best features.

The night I met David, he was so cute and humorous that I couldn't help but smile at him; I'm sure that's why he asked me to dance. As we danced, I smiled and laughed at his lively, animated dance steps. I wasn't surprised in the least when he asked for my phone number and offered a dinner invitation for the following week."

Lyle and Delores

A woman's smile is her beacon of influence. It adds a sparkle to her eyes, softness to her face and an alluring aura that causes a man to pause, look and think about her.

Lyle, a 49-year-old business owner, "I was shopping for a new skillet at a kitchen supply store, when this attractive woman who was standing about 10 feet away looked at me and made eye contact; she smiled and then casually looked away. Inside I blushed; I was almost certain that she was flirting with me. I told myself, 'Lyle, don't let this opportunity get away. Smile back at her and see what happens.' Sure enough when I smiled at her, she smiled back and then said a soft, 'Hello.' As far as I was concerned that was the green light I was looking for. 'Excuse me,' I said. 'Do you know anything about Teflon skillets?'"

Delores, "It's true, I was expressing an interest in Lyle when I smiled at him that day in the kitchenware store. I've always thought it would be wonderful to be with a man who wanted to share the experience of cooking and conversation.

When Lyle spoke to me I couldn't have been more delighted. We talked for twenty minutes about the best pots and pans, cooking techniques and our favorite foods, when we realized that we lived only a few miles apart. That's when we decided to exchange e-mail addresses. Two weeks later I put together a small dinner party with the intention of inviting Lyle as my guest. That was eight months ago and today we are cookin' on all four burners and hosting some of the best Cajun dinner parties on the Bayou.

Smile and the World Smiles With You.
Frown and Watch Your Date Take You Home Early.

Leave the Frown at Home

Women go out with hopes of meeting a wonderful man. And what do they do when they get there? They sit around trying to look smart, chic and cute—*the three things that men fear most.* Or, worse yet, they frown and appear unfriendly, aloof or uptight—*the three things that men avoid most.*

A frowning face mirrors a frowning attitude. If you are unhappy and discontent on the inside, you will be unable to mask it on the outside with a half-baked smile.

A genuine smile is difficult to fake. It is a broad, open expression that comes from the heart and shines through the eyes. A smile portrays pleasure, amusement and interest, and reflects friendliness, sincerity and warmth.

A true smile can coax a man out of his comfort zone and put him into *your* world.

Sprucing Up Your Curb Appeal

24

A woman's outward appearance is part of the man-hunting package.

*I*t's time to discuss the Ultimate Husband Hunter's visual bait—*or* in real estate terms—a woman's "curb appeal."

Think of yourself as a homeowner. You have placed your house on the market and have high hopes that your house will bring top dollar. But, as any real estate agent will tell you, if the house is not well maintained and attractive on the outside, it will not have the kind of *curb appeal* that will encourage a prospective buyer to investigate the possibilities on the inside.

While you are busy checking out the appearance and qualifications of a man, be aware that he is sizing up you as well.

Men are the same darn way! A Quality Man is not going to be interested in pursuing a woman who does not take the time and effort to fix up her physical appearance. A woman, who is sincerely interested in increasing her odds of finding a wonderful QM, needs to consider the different ways in which she can improve her overall personal appearance.

"79% of men on a first date take 15 minutes to determine whether or not they want to see a woman again," states It's Just Lunch dating service.

The Proverbial Fashion Rut

First impressions are lasting impressions. Sad as it is, a man may not take the time to get to know a woman who doesn't present an attractive visual presence. *Shallow?* Perhaps. But it's a fact of life and it isn't going to change.

The way a woman dresses reveals a lot about the way she feels about herself.

Sometimes fashion eludes a woman. Perhaps she never learned a good sense of style or it's never been a priority for her. Maybe her personal appearance took a back seat to her career, family responsibilities and household chores. Years later it doesn't occur to her that she has taken on a look that is outdated, frumpy or unattractive.

I was 40-years-old when I began my cosmetics career. It was my introduction to the image industry. I started by experimenting with cosmetics and skincare products that literally erased years from my face. I learned how to choose clothing styles and colors that made me look slimmer and more attractive. I budgeted for regular manicures; I got a chic new hair cut and lightened my color. I visited my dentist to purchase a bleaching system for my teeth and repaired the chip in my front tooth. It took a lot of time and effort to redefine my image and I consider it be the wisest investment I ever made.

What Is "Image" and Is It Really That Important?

Image is the mental picture we have of someone or something. For example, a woman in a tailored silk suit, stylish Chanel reading glasses, studying *The Wall Street Journal* while sipping on a latte at a downtown bistro, could give the impression of a lawyer, corporate executive or investment banker. A couple of tables away at the same bistro, another woman clad in pink cotton scrubs, tennis shoes, long hair pulled back in a ponytail, no visible makeup, wolfing down a hot dog and beer may give the impression that she is in the medical or dental field . . . or does she clean houses for a living? Image may not be everything; nevertheless, it gives one a perceived value for a person.

Self-Image Tip

Never compare yourself (your accomplishments, possessions or appearance) to another woman. Yes, find yourself a positive role model to emulate, but comparing your self-worth with that of another is self-esteem suicide. Time is better spent identifying and developing your unique qualities and talents. You may be surprised to discover that you are smarter, more clever, humorous or creative, even prettier, than most of the women you know.

Self-image, on the other hand, is how one perceives oneself, based on one's accomplishments, qualities and personal worth; what one thinks others think of them, and last, but certainly not least, how one presents oneself by her physical appearance.

If a woman is unhappy with the way she looks, she will project a poor self-image. A poor self-image is largely responsible for a woman's low self-esteem and lack of confidence.

What Good Is a Mirror If the Woman Looking Into It Does Not Change the Things She Sees?

Dr. Phil McGraw says, "It's time to get real." I say, "It's time to take an honest look at the way others see us."

A woman's most important self-improvement work needs to begin on the inside; however, never underestimate the significance of a well-groomed outside appearance. Until a woman is willing to be completely honest about her outward presentation, she cannot even begin to make the needed improvements to her overall image.

What can a woman see in a mirror once the blinders come off? She might see hair that is lackluster, straggly, in need of styling, teeth that are a bit dingy, out-of-date eyeglasses that are visibly scratched, sweat suits for a wardrobe, non-existent makeup, or a remnant of spinach in her front tooth leftover from lunch. Yes, I may be exaggerating a bit, but any one these "image busters" can dampen a man's interest.

Now that I have your attention, here is an abbreviated lesson on how-to improve your overall personal appearance.

Seven-Step Image Formula

1. **Color Analysis:** Colors can make a dramatic difference in the way a woman looks and feels. Flattering colors, whether in clothing or cosmetics, are especially important around a woman's face. The *wrong colors* can make a woman look drab and older, while the *right colors* can make her appear younger, cheerful and vibrant. Seek out an experienced cosmetics consultant or knowledgeable clothing salesperson to assist you with your best colors.

The Truth Is, Most Women Think That Their Best Clothing Color is Black!

Warm and Cool Color Tip:
As a general rule, color coordinate your total look (cosmetics, clothing and accessories) within the same color tones. The cool colors are pink, purple, blue, blue-red and emerald green. The warm colors are peach, coral, yellow, orange-red, lime and khaki.

2. **Body Shape:** Stand in front of a full-length mirror and study your body shape. Decide if you most resemble an hourglass, rectangle, triangle or wedge, and then wear only those clothing styles that best flatter your body shape. I call it "body illusion." Accentuate your best physical assets, camouflage your body's imperfections and learn to love and accept the rest. A woman can look ten pounds heavier or ten pounds lighter depending on the clothing styles she wears.

Body Shape Tip:
Visit the lingerie department for the newest in body contour under-garments. Bra minimizers provide lift and visual diminishment for the full-busted woman, while body smoothers hold in the tummy, thighs and buttocks. And you thought you needed to go on a diet!

3. **Core Wardrobing:** Approach your wardrobe with a discerning, critical eye. Your goal is to eliminate the clothes from your closet that (1) do not fit properly (2) are unflattering in color, or (3) are out-of-date. If you are willing to tailor your ill-fitting clothes—*fine!* Otherwise get rid of them.

A Confused Closet Will Only Confuse Its Owner.

Now, get to work on organizing your closet. Separate your clothes by season (spring/summer and fall/winter), warm and cool colors, and then by pieces (blouses, slacks, skirts, vests, jackets and suits). You are laying a foundation for a working wardrobe that will "mix-and-match" to create a variety of attractive outfits.

"Women wear only 20% of their clothing 80% of the time," says OrgangizedHome.com. That tells me to get rid of the 80% that is taking up valuable space in your closet.

Gradually replenish your wardrobe with a few "quality clothes" that you will love and wear forever. Remember, purchasing clothing that is not in your best colors, that does not flatter your body shape, and that does not compliment your "mix and match" wardrobing strategy is a *big waste of money!*

Wardrobing Tip:
One really nice white blouse contributes more to a woman's
self-esteem than a closet full of clothes. One great pair of shoes
can make a woman feel special. And if she feels special, she
can pull it off in a $24.00 pair of jeans.

4. **Fashion Personality:** Your personality plays an important role in the fashion statement you want to develop for yourself. The four fashion personalities are: Natural, Classic, Romantic and Dramatic. Understanding your fashion personality will help you to create a look that you love and are comfortable with as well as avoiding future clothing mistakes.

5. **Accessorizing:** Accessories are anything that you add to your wardrobe to give it a special touch. It is the essence of style: belts, jewelry, scarves, purses, hats, patterned hosiery and shoes can turn any outfit into a fashion statement.

Facial Tip:
Your eyeglasses are a fashion accessory, too.
And if your frames are out-of-style . . .
you are out-of-style as well!

6. **Personal Grooming:** Some grooming habits are obvious, such as bathing regularly, shaving your underarms and legs, using deodorant and brushing your teeth. However, here are some grooming tips that every woman should take to heart.

a. **Face:** Whether it's fine lines and wrinkles or bumps and zits, visit your favorite skincare counter to purchase a regimen that will benefit your skin type. While you are there, book an appointment for a full cosmetics makeover that will familiarize you with the cosmetics products and colors that will enhance your natural beauty. *Most department store cosmetics counters are more than happy to offer you a free makeover, or a makeover with a minimum purchase.*

b. **Teeth:** Go to the mirror right now and take a close look at your teeth. *What do you see?* Are your teeth stained, crooked or chipped? Is there a buildup of unsightly tartar? Then ask yourself, *"Are you turned off by a man's ragged, discolored teeth?"*

Dental Tip:
Visit your dentist twice a year to have your teeth cleaned—especially if you are a smoker, coffee or red wine drinker. Invest in a professional or over-the-counter bleaching product that will whiten your teeth. If your teeth are in need of straightening or veneers, consider doing it. Don't underestimate the value of attractive, clean teeth.

c. **Body:** Be kind to your body with baths, lotions and perfumes. It will awaken your femininity, as well as, arouse his masculinity. Find your signature fragrance among the many sample perfume bottles at the department store and always have it handy at home or in your purse.

d. **Hands and Feet:** *Stop biting those nails!* Either give yourself regular manicures and pedicures, or schedule regular appointments with a nail care professional. Men really do notice a woman's finger and toe nails.

Skin Tip:
Women, and men, are often unaware that they have dry,
rough skin. It's a real turnoff to finally hold someone's hand
only to discover it feels like an alligator's paw. Get in the
habit of using hand cream to moisturize your parched, dry
skin and then keep a small tube in your purse for an
emergency touch-up.

7. **Hairstyle:** If you haven't had your hair styled in two years, it's time to make an appointment. A great haircut and a good color can take years off your appearance. Look at the women whose hair styles you admire, and ask for their stylist's name and number.

Hair Advice:
If your stylist refuses to cut your hair the way you
want it, or she continually turns your hair red, gold or
green—and it's not supposed to be that color—
ditch the loyalty and switch to another stylist.

It takes honesty, time, effort and money to take care of one's appearance. It's the woman who is smart enough to do the most with her attitude, intelligence and outward appearance that catches a man's eye.

Taking Care of Yourself

*T*hus far, *Secrets of the Ultimate Husband Hunter* has promoted a Love-All-Men philosophy to help a woman attract, date and win the heart of her Dream Man. The only way a woman can attract the *Right Man* is to be the *Right Woman*, one who appreciates and respects the individuality of others. Now let's talk about how to value and respect ourselves as women. How do we go about it?

We Are Our Own Most Valuable Possession

A man can tell when a woman respects herself. He senses the woman with strong personal boundaries, and the woman who is a submissive, compliant pushover. He knows that he will have to esteem the self-respecting woman, if he wants to be with her. As for the submissive, compliant pushover . . . the principled man will avoid her, while the unprincipled man will take advantage of her.

Tender Loving Care for Y-O-U

It is a turning point in a woman's life when she realizes that understanding a man is not nearly as crucial as understanding herself.

- Learn to *accept* and *appreciate* a wider variety of people and you will learn to accept, love and honor your own uniqueness. This is a monumental step to *taking care of yourself.*

- Always be *alert* and *cautious* when meeting and dating men. Be aware of your surroundings. Never hesitate to leave your date if he displays questionable or bad behavior. Your safety, health and well-being are your top priority.

- Listen to your *intuition!* Trust your *instincts!* This will help you make decisions that are in *YOUR* best interest.

- Take time to *discover* who you are, and then love what you discover. Decide what's important to you and pursue it.

- Work continually on the multi-facets of your self-improvement plan, whether it be reading, counseling, journaling, spirituality or talking with a girlfriend.

- Treat men, and everyone, in a *caring, honest, respectful manner* because that is how you expect to be treated. Surround yourself with people who display those same characteristics.

- Stand up for your *values* and *beliefs*; do not tolerate behavior from men that goes against those standards.

- Realize that you are *complete without a man.* Learn to enjoy your company first and you will find it much easier to enjoy a man's company.

- Take time to take care of your needs first. Spend time with your friends, because your friends will still be around after your dysfunctional man is long gone.
- *Avoid* hurtful, dysfunctional relationships.
- *Respect* your mind, body and soul. Never subjugate your needs to a man's demands.

In everything you think, say and do, learn to take care of yourself!

Part Five

Avoiding the Pitfalls of Dating

"There are two kinds of mistakes: The ones we keep making and suffer from, and the ones we learn from and avoid."

—Nancy Nichols

Shooting Yourself in the Foot

26

*I*t has happened to every woman who has ever gone out on a date: He was witty, charming and fun to be with, and from every indication he had a great time, too. He tenderly held her hand during the movie. He gave her a passionate goodnight kiss at the door and told her, "I'll call you next week." Next week came, but the phone call never did.

"What happened?" "What went wrong?" Or, even worse— "Did *I* do something wrong?" she asks herself.

Many times she did nothing wrong, but there were times that she committed a dating blunder or relationship *faux pas* . . . and he never called again. Her aim was to be a confident, charming woman but, instead, she said the wrong thing or she behaved in an unattractive manner shooting herself in the foot. Be careful to avoid the *Pitfalls of Dating*.

Checklist of Dating Blunders:

❑ **Falling in Love Too Fast.** Romanticizing, fantasizing and reading between the lines can run off a *QM*. Ignoring or making excuses for his bad behavior can allow the *Wrong Man* into your life.

❏ **Controlling, Manipulating Behavior.** Men avoid a controlling woman! A man would rather take his chances confronting a pack of rabid dogs, than to deal with an over-bearing, bossy woman.

❏ **Clingy, Needy, Insecure Behavior.** Equally scary to a man is a needy, insecure woman. Neediness will scare him away while insecurity can attract an abusive, controlling man.

❏ **Fearful, Self-Protecting Behavior** can cause a woman to appear unfriendly and aloof. A woman may block the development of a relationship if she is uncomfortable with a man's interest, paralyzed at the thought of intimacy, or afraid to show her interest in him.

❏ **Using a Human Measuring Stick.** Judging and criticizing others will make you appear distasteful and unattractive.

❏ **Losing Your "Mystery."** Filling the conversational void with too much personal information—too soon—can squelch a man's desire to pursue a woman.

❏ **Calling and Chasing a Man.** Out of eagerness or insecurity a woman will impulsively call a man, rather than waiting for him to call her—first!

❏ **Caving Into Sex Too Soon** can short-circuit an otherwise promising relationship.

❏ **Talking About Money.** He will be cautious when a woman's biggest interest seems to be how much money he has.

❏ **Dating for Money or Position.** A woman who marries for money or position may later find herself looking for the love and intimacy that was never present at the beginning of the relationship.

❏ **Dating and Marrying a Father Figure.** A woman who looks for love, approval and shelter in a father figure, may be disappointed later when he is unable to fulfill her unrealistic emotional expectations.

❏ **Prematurely Traveling Together.** Generally, unless you are ready to sleep with a man . . . don't go!

❏ **Drinking Too Much.** Don't try to convince yourself that you *"didn't act stupid"* when you drank—*when truthfully, you did.* Drinking too much can wreck your chances with a *QM*, along with your BMW.

❏ **Boasting About the Men in Your Past.** No man wants to compete with men from your past—*dead or alive.*

❏ **Bragging and Boasting About Yourself** screams conceit and insecurity.

❏ **Talking Negatively About Anyone** will only be a bad reflection on you.

❏ **Trying to Fix a Man.** Be sure that you like him *exactly* the way he is—*now!* And what you don't like, you must be willing to live with. There is much misery in trying to change a man.

Any one of these nasty behaviors can cause a man to think twice about the woman he is dating. Two can cause him to pause and step back. Three or more can cause him to run into the street yelling and screaming—**"TAXI!"**

If you are unsure if any of this behavior describes you—ask a friend. But be ready to hear the truth.

Don't Be a Needa Man

Meet my friend—Needa Man. She *r-e-a-l-l-y* needs a man.

By day Needa fantasizes about having a man to talk to, care for and share experiences with. He is someone with whom she can build a secure and romantic future. At night Needa dreams of him lying next to her in bed, protecting and comforting her with the warmth of his body. The next morning, when she awakens, her elaborate man-fantasy begins again.

Needa has spent her entire life wanting and needing a man. Her every thought and movement revolves around having a man. She can't enjoy the present because her life is full of unhappiness and uncertainty. She fears her future because she's afraid she can't make it on her own. Needa feels incomplete *without a man in her life.*

Needa's problem is that she mistakenly believes that a man is the cure for her loneliness and insecurity. But she will never find a man to fill the void of her needy, demanding soul, because no man can keep up with her constant requirement for reassurance and attention.

Bonnie, a twice divorced 48-year-old property manager: "I saw Tom out and about in the single scene for years. One night at a party he finally asked me out.

Our first date seemed to blossom quickly into a relationship. Tom told me he was looking for a special woman to be in his life and that he was falling for me. He talked about our future plans together and he helped with my small house repairs. I thought I had finally found a man whom I could trust and love.

From the beginning, I knew that Tom wanted to sleep with me; I told him that I was not ready for sexual intimacy. But he kept talking his talk and pushing my needy, co-dependent buttons. After a week and a half I gave in. Three days later he broke a date with me, claiming he was sick. Two days after that he dumped me over the phone. I had been set-up, ambushed and disposed of like the evening trash.

Men Know How to Play a Pinball Machine and They Know How to Push a Needy Woman's Buttons.

How did I mishandle this relationship? I was too nice, too accommodating and too willing to give up my personal power. When Tom called for a date at the last minute, even though I was tired and wanted to stay at home, I went out to please him. Next, I gave away my "mystery" by giving him my cell number so he could reach me while I was out with my girlfriends. Finally, because he had fixed my closet door, I felt obligated to take dinner to him the night he was "supposedly" sick and broke our date. Tom never had a chance to pursue me, because I did all the work.

At first I was heartbroken by Tom's deceitful treatment . . . then I was enraged. What *really* hurt was that I *knew* I had run Tom off with my needy words and actions. So desperate was I for his love and approval, I let him enter my heart and my bedroom. The next morning I opened my eyes and he was gone."

Running Men Off

Needa's greatest talent is running men off. Men could have been in a relationship with her but chose not to because she was helpless, clinging and needy.

A Man Can Smell a Needy Woman's Agenda Quicker Than He Can Smell Prime Rib.

It is natural for a man to be attracted to a woman who needs his love, affection and support, but excessive neediness is a very **un**-attractive trait. A man will pull way from an affection-starved woman and become cautious and resistant if he suspects her main objective is security. Either way, a QM is likely to disappear.

Jared, "Needing a man is not that bad in a guy's world, unless it is excessive neediness.

Let's say that a man has just started dating a woman and he discovers that she gets upset when he doesn't call her every day, she pouts when he doesn't hold her hand when they walk down the street, or she becomes irrationally jealous when he speaks to another woman. The average man is probably not going to press for a relationship with this woman. A week later he discovers that she doesn't pay her bills on time, she's $20,000.00 in debt and yet she spends her weekends power shopping at the mall. For the average man, this could be a deal-breaker.

A Man Does Not Want to Work Overtime to Satisfy a Woman's Abnormal Emotional Needs or Exorbitant Spending Habits.

There may be some men whose sentimental hearts and big wallets would take on this woman's excessive emotional and financial baggage, but more likely than not, her neediness will send most men running to the hills."

Committing to the Wrong Man

Needa's other talent is committing to the *Wrong Man*, a man who is hurtful and dysfunctional. *Why?* Because her *"need-a-man"* cravings overpower her intuition and common sense, and her low self-esteem tells her that she is undeserving of a Quality Man. Once she is in a harmful relationship she remains in it, because she's afraid that no one better will come along.

Marilyn a 39-year-old divorced department store clerk and mother of two small children was looking for a man to rescue her. But when she found him . . . what a price she had to pay!

Marilyn could barely make ends meet on her small hourly salary. Her ex-husband, a construction worker, didn't pay the bills while they were married, and after they divorced she couldn't count on him for support.

It had been three years since Marilyn's divorce; she struggled with loneliness and the exhausting challenge of raising her children alone. She felt certain she would have remarried by now, but alas, she just couldn't seem to make it down the aisle. Then she met Sonny.

Sonny was a sales clerk in the men's department of the store where she worked. He was interested in Marilyn, but she was certain that Sonny lacked the qualities she truly wanted in a man. But Marilyn was companionless and lonely, so she consented to go to dinner with him. Then she went to more dinners. Then he helped her by picking up her children from school. Before she knew it, he was spending the night at her small apartment.

In the beginning Sonny appeared to be a considerate and caring man. He even loaned Marilyn $900.00 to pay her overdue rent. Shortly thereafter, he began to maliciously berate her about her past relationships with other men. Then one night, he lost his temper and struck her violently across the face. Marilyn began to experience first-hand Sonny's controlling, contemptuous behavior; something she had suspected was there all along.

Marilyn allowed herself to enter a relationship that was less than she deserved from the very beginning. She was looking for a man to rescue her and when the right man didn't show up, she settled for Sonny out of desperation. It took six months of Sonny's verbal and physical abuse before Marilyn finally got the courage to get rid of him and resign herself to being alone again.

The tell-tale behavior of a needy woman:

- Chasing a man *first*
- Being too *available*
- Subjugating her *needs* in a relationship
- Giving in too *quickly* to a man's sexual desires

Every time a needy woman's relationship fails . . . her desperation for a man's love increases. Now, turn the page. It's time to meet Needa's equally dysfunctional sister—*Scaredy-Cat Girl.*

28
Scaredy-Cat Girl

Scaredy-Cat Girl is afraid of making a mistake, of saying or doing the wrong thing. She's afraid to stand up for her beliefs and ask for the things she wants and needs in life. She's afraid that if a man really gets to know her, he won't like what he sees. She's afraid of being unloved, being alone or being left behind. She's afraid. She's afraid. And she doesn't know how to stop being afraid.

She's a bona fide, certifiable, pedigreed *Scaredy-Cat Girl.* Someone, at sometime, taught her that she was not worthy of the love and respect that a woman needs and deserves.

It's hard to believe that there are women like this among us—but they are in the millions, and their emotional pain is very deep and very real. They feel flawed and inferior and they live in fear that their inadequacies will be discovered.

Feeling "less-than-others" is a debilitating mindset that beats a woman's self-esteem to a pulp. It is a state-of-mind which stands between her and the things she wants most in life.

Not everyone will understand the insecure, perplexed mind of a Scaredy-Cat Girl. In the past she was criticized for her thoughts, requests or actions by a loved one or an authority figure. She was taught to subjugate her wants, needs and desires to the demands of others. The result . . . she learned to expect rejection and displeasure, to repress her feelings and to fear the word "no!" *Deny . . . numb . . . and bury . . .* that's how she copes with life.

A Recipe for Loneliness

When I was a young woman in my twenties, my low self-esteem was so extreme that I was uncomfortable going to lunch with men and women alike. Whereas a cocktail at dinner brought out the social butterfly in me, being at a business or social luncheon without the buffer of a merlot, tapped into my extreme feelings of insecurity and inadequacy. The sad truth was that I felt different . . . as if there were something wrong with me . . . as if I didn't fit in with normal people.

I was afraid I wasn't attractive enough. I was afraid that I couldn't pull off an intelligent conversation. I was afraid someone would ask me a personal question that would expose my defects. I was afraid to ask someone else a personal question because I feared they would think I was prying. The only way I knew to avoid my luncheon anxieties was to decline an invitation using lots of lame excuses.

The truth was, there was nothing wrong with me: I was attractive. I received an average education that helped me to land an above average job. I had a nice car and apartment, girlfriends to run with and guys to occasionally date. Why then did I feel so flawed?

My life had been a hodge-podge of critical influences that not only destroyed my self-confidence, but sent me on a path of fear and uncertainty. To mask my imagined deficiencies I developed self-protective behavior which resulted in the disinterest, displeasure or rejection from others. Sometimes I would withdraw to avoid people; other times I was overly sensitive or defensive. It seemed that most of my friendships were superficial.

In other words, if I looked in a mirror and frowned, the mirror would surely frown back at me. For twenty-five years my fear of rejection and disapproval caused me to push away potentially rewarding relationships—with both men and women.

Untrusting and Uncertain of Men

Scaredy-Cat Girl could have turned out to be a confident, self-reliant woman (a woman who knows who she is, what she wants and is unafraid to go after it) . . . but she didn't, because the negative influences of her past stunted her emotional development. Her fearful nature caused her to constantly worry about what a man was thinking and what he wanted. She yearned for an intimate relationship, but she feared that if he got too close, he may have seen the inferiority that existed deep within her soul.

Selena, a 41-year-old executive secretary, "Kenny is the nicest man I've been out with in a very long time. Right from the start he acted as if he liked me, but I was scared that I would do something stupid and run him off.

My problem with men has always been my acute fear of rejection. I'm afraid to let a guy get to know me, because I'm afraid he'll see my insecurities and lose respect for me.

Or, if I let a guy know how much I really like him, he'll lose interest and stop dating me. So I play it safe, which I am told, makes me appear aloof and disinterested."

In the beginning Kenny genuinely liked Selena, but when he couldn't break through her icy armor, he became frustrated and pulled away.

Selena allowed her unfounded fears to come between her and a potentially loving relationship. From the beginning, she felt unworthy of Kenny's interest and affection causing her to fear his rejection. To protect herself from being hurt, she subconsciously discouraged his pursuit. And Kenny felt rejected, broke up with her and went back to his old girlfriend. Once again, Selena shielded her fragile ego by trying to convince herself that Kenny was still in love with his old flame. The fact was, he really wanted a relationship with Selena but, instead, he returned to the woman that required less work.

Worry is Taking a Negative Thought and Thinking About it Over and Over Again.

A woman who constantly worries about "what a man is thinking" will feel self-doubt and practice self-protection, both of which will impede the development of intimacy between herself and a man.

The Words of Insecure, Fearful Women

- "After years of marriage, I am now divorced; I'm not sure that a man would even be attracted to me."

- "I can't seem to get beyond my fear of being alone. I'm afraid I won't find a husband. I'm afraid one day I'll fall through the cracks and become a bag lady."
- "I have extremely low self-esteem . . . that's why I allow losers into my life; they don't threaten me."
- "I commit my emotions to a man way too soon and then find myself stuck in the wrong relationship."
- "I'm afraid of making the wrong decision. I'm afraid to be me."

Yes, Scaredy-Cat Girl lives in fear that someone will hurt her. What she doesn't realize, however, is that her fear of rejection and abandonment has a way of becoming reality. Thus, the life she lives in fear is worse punishment than any other person could ever inflict on her.

29
Good-Bye Needa Man and Scaredy-Cat Girl

The Experiences in Life That Hurt You Can Also Heal You.

It is the culmination of our lifetime of experiences—*good, bad and indifferent*—that make us who we are today. The experiences that hurt us the most—*the ones we survived emotionally*—can inspire us to correct our flawed thoughts, beliefs and behavior that impede our ability to be self-reliant individuals.

A Child Is Born With a Perfect Spirit

When a child is born she is given a spirit that is playful, creative, inquisitive and unafraid; she enters the world with unlimited love and trust. It is intended that all children develop their traits of strength and character to take them into adulthood, and that this strength and character make a positive impact on the people who come into their lives. Not so for *Needa Man* and *Scaredy-Cat*

Girl, for the people and circumstances in their lives taught them fear, doubt, rejection and mistrust.

> *The negative things that happen to a child will influence the way she interprets her world as an adult.*

As a young girl, I remember struggling to find my place in life. I grew up sandwiched between two brothers, in a neighborhood of all boys, with an emotionally absent dad and a mother having to work outside the home. I started out early having to defend my female rights.

Today I proudly call myself a "scrapper," because I've always had to fight for everything I've achieved in life. As an adolescent, I fought to prove myself a worthy tomboy among the neighborhood kids. In high school and college I struggled with making good grades, my dating insecurities and the cliques of popular women. As an adult, I withstood the hardships of dysfunctional relationships, failed marriages, divorces, and the challenge of raising two small children on a single mother's salary.

> *The Experiences That Hurt You the Most Can Also Make You the Strongest.*

*My years of harsh experiences did much to damage my self-esteem and confidence. Then one day I realized that the mistakes and misfortunes of my past were the **very things** that could give me the wisdom, confidence and courage that I had hungered for all my life.*

Change is a Cognitive Choice; So is Forgiving and Releasing the Painful Experiences of Our Past.

I thought, "Yes, my negative past and the mistakes I made have impaired the quality of my life. I wished that parts of my life had turned out differently, but that was not the case. The decision I needed to make was: do I continue to make the same mistakes, and do I allow my hurtful past to affect my future?"

If I choose to drag the baggage of my past around with me, I will be responsible for the disappointing events of my future.

"Quit thinking about all the things I did wrong," I told myself, and instead, from this moment forward think, ***"What can I do differently?"***

Do not dwell on all that you are NOT, instead, concentrate on the positive aspects of what YOU ARE!

I began to identify my personal strengths. This is what I discovered:

- The painful consequences of my dysfunctional past led me to seek help from self-improvement books and counseling; from this I gained understanding and wisdom.
- My feelings of being unloved, neglected and mistreated throughout my life taught me to be caring and sensitive to the feelings of others.
- The judgmental and unkind actions of others taught me patience and compassion.

- My inability to express my true feelings motivated me to develop effective communication skills; I learned how to relate, ask for the things I needed and set personal boundaries.

- I discovered that my struggles to make good grades in school stemmed from my limited ability to mentally retain facts and figures; I learned to be disciplined and tenacious in order to achieve my scores.

- As an adult, I realized that I was a highly visual person, and for me to remember information, it had to be reinforced visually; this lead me to develop my analytical skills and creative talents.

- My lack of finances as a single parent made me determined to educate myself and find a job with above average earnings. From this I learned to be pro-active, self-motivated and assertive.

Once my personal inventory was complete I came to realize that not only was I okay, *I was more than okay.* I was astonished at the caliber of talents and qualities that I was born with and developed over the years. For the first time in my life I felt complete and competent.

My life has been a honing experience, "the gift that came in an ugly package," I say. But I survived. I overcame. And I evolved into an intelligent, caring, accomplished woman. I believe I never would have achieved the depth and breadth of who I am today without the adverse events of my life.

What a Woman Believes, She Can Also Become

As a child, I remember being animated, creative, affectionate, head-strong and fearless. I recall the bright, happy smile that attracted the attention of those around me and my inquisitive nature that led me to make new friends, climb the tallest trees and attempt the more difficult recipes in my mother's cookbook. I loved to draw, paint and sew. I swiftly rode my bicycle, played dress-up with my dolls, and I was proud that I could take down a much older 5' 7" seventh grade boy in a rough game of tackle football. When night came, I would lay my head in my mother's lap, exhausted, as she lovingly brushed my hair.

I was a vibrant little girl with an incredible zest for life and as an adult I believed that regardless of my past, those characteristics were still alive inside me. For that reason, I can be a complete and beautiful woman. The only thing that was standing between me and that realization was my negative mindset.

There is always an excuse to stay in the past. Tell me, what's a good excuse for not moving on to a better future?

The Cure

I was afraid to stand up for my beliefs and ask for the things I wanted and needed in life.

Camille once told me, "Every woman deserves to be put on a pedestal and I would never consider a man who did not treat me that way."

Once again, Camille's crass, narcissistic nature shines through, **but** *in her selfish logic I heard the emancipating words, "A woman deserves the best that life has to offer." Camille got the best out of life because she believed that she* **deserved** *it; she* **asked** *for it; and she* **held out** *until she got it.*

I, on the other hand, was programmed to accept the hurtful words and behavior of others . . . and the more I accepted

. . . the more undeserving I felt . . . and the more undeserving I felt . . . the more dysfunctional I became.

*And then . . . just like that . . . I got mad! "You deserve the good things in life, too!" I told myself. "**Toughen-up you wimp! You are the cake . . . not the crumbs!**" I got mad! I got smart! That's when I quit dating losers and abusers and began to date men who deserved me.*

There is not a woman alive who does not want to be confident and self-reliant . . . if only she thought she could.

Life is no fun when you are needy and insecure, continually seeking the love, approval and support of a man. Once again I stress, go to counseling, group discussions and spiritual worship. Journal and read self-help books. Surround yourself with supportive, caring people who will help you move away from the negative thoughts and dysfunctional behavior that rob you of the *best-that-life-has-to-offer!*

Survival 30 *Tips for the Needy, Fearful Woman*

*I*n a heart to heart talk, Rachael Ray talk show host and cooking guru, told her desperately dating audience:

"I didn't get married till I was thirty-seven. I've had more than one best-selling book . . . five television shows . . . and do you know why I got all that stuff? I didn't think about men. I went to work and I focused on me and what I wanted out of life."

Right on, Rach! Concentrating on your career, *your* hobbies and what would make *your* life more exciting will bring out the best in *you!*

Your Personal Checklist:

❏ Identify and honor *YOUR* wants and needs in a relationship. Never defer to the unreasonable demands of others.

❏ Don't be afraid of confrontation. Learn to trust your intuition about what you are feeling and stand up for yourself by expressing those feelings.

❏ Reject and remove yourself from the dysfunctional behavior of others. Learn to turn a deaf ear and walk away from hurtful comments and controlling demands. Every time you do, it is a deliberate step toward self-reliance.

❏ Maintain a regular social life that doesn't include a man. Go out with your female friends and concentrate on enjoying their company. Put your romantic longings on hold when you are with them.

❏ It's okay to date more than one man at a time. *Why* is this significant? Not only will it build your self-confidence, it will take the romantic focus off "one man."

❏ Learn to enjoy your own company. Spend time alone and surround yourself with the things you enjoy most—silk pajamas and a good novel in front a warm fireplace, the scent of vanilla candles burning in the kitchen, or a shrimp remoulade and a glass of champagne while watching your favorite movie. Pamper yourself without feeling guilty.

❏ A pet is a wonderful source of unconditional love. Visit your local humane society . . . you may wind up adopting each other.

❏ Enjoy dating for the sake of entertainment and friendship. Dating in hopes of a serious relationship is an unrewarding process.

❏ Never underestimate a man's ability to do the calling, asking and pursuing. Give him a chance to show you what he can do.

❏ Stop worrying and waiting for a man to call you. Tell yourself, "You are the prize and he will be lucky if you answer the phone." When he calls, don't cancel your plans to accommodate him.

❏ When a man doesn't call you right away, don't assume there is something wrong with you. He could be busy or waiting for a reason (or the right time) to call. If he doesn't call: (1) it wasn't the right chemistry (not a good reason to beat yourself up), or (2) maybe there's something wrong with *him*—*and not you!*

❏ Don't romanticize or fanaticize about a man. Realize that everything he says or does in the early stages of dating (his attention, flattery, flowers, romantic dinners and constant emails) . . . is nothing more than *sweet-talk!*

❏ Pay no attention to the tingling, throbbing, love-sick feelings that you experience about a new man. Understand that it's a natural part of your Needa-Man cravings.

❏ Learn to turn loose of a man, mentally and physically, for a day, a week or longer. When he happily and willingly comes back to you, you will experience a surge of confidence and self-worth.

❏ Tell yourself, "It's nice to have a man. Want one. But don't need one if he's a dysfunctional man."

❏ In the early stages of a relationship, calling a man can make you appear anxious. Anxiety will make you appear needy. If you have to guess whether or not to call . . . the answer is "don't call!"

❏ If the man you are dating suddenly seems unavailable, take care of your mental state by making yourself slightly more unavailable. It's better to do this than to call him and later wish you hadn't.

❏ Caving in to your romantic longings in the early stages of a relationship (whether it's calling and chasing a man, or succumbing to sexual advances) will further fuel your neediness. Remaining true to yourself, doing what's best for you, will heal your needy nature.

❏ If the lack of money is your biggest fear, *then do something about it!* Knock the dust off your resume and begin looking for a better job. If a formal education is holding you back, bite the bullet and go back to school. Your choices are: (1) Five years from now you can have a degree and the security of a higher paying job, or (2) you can be five years older and still be struggling to pay your bills. *Which will it be?*

❏ Finally, never, never, ever compare yourself to another woman. It will only chip away at your confidence and self-worth.

Needa Man and *Scaredy-Cat Girl* . . . get your self-reliant act together and get the love, respect and happiness you so richly deserve.

31

Don't Be Giving
the Squirrel Away

A squirrel is one of the most difficult game animals to hunt. They're fast-thinking, rapid-moving, agile and extremely clever. They swiftly sprint up a tree, quickly leap from limb to limb, camouflage themselves within the forest landscape, and then without warning—*they disappear.*

Men hunt squirrels because it is a stimulating, exciting, fun sport. Like a squirrel, a smart and designing single woman should offer a man no less of a challenge during the "chase."

A male friend once told me, "There are two dominant sources of power in the world. One is wealth. The other is sex. Men typically use wealth to get the things they want in life. While women—knowingly or unknowingly—use sex as their tool of manipulation and control."

Camille in her consistent shameless style, said, *"Give-the-squirrel-away* too soon and you give away your bargaining power. Unless a wedding ring and a nice house are on the horizon, a woman needs to keep the squirrel in the cage."

Once again, *ya' gotta love her*—because she's **right!** It was Camille's tough attitude of **Quit-Giving-Away-Your-Most-Valuable-Resource** that kept men from using and abusing her, and kept them eagerly pursuing her. Camille got what she wanted from a man because she fully understood that—*SEX is more valuable the FIRST time!*

A Man's Job Is to Bring Home His Dream Woman

Men were born to control and conquer the world. They were designed to achieve an environment of activity, comfort and safety. They will go out into the world to strategically acquire the things that bring them intellectual stimulation, emotional fulfillment and physical satisfaction.

One of the roles of a woman is to help a man enjoy the varied aspects of his life. She shares his aspirations; she applauds his goals and accomplishments; she takes comfort in his protection, affection and support. It is her presence and acceptance which helps him experience his identity and enjoy the pleasures of his senses. For that reason, a man is compelled to seek out, woo and win his Dream Woman. Pursuing a woman for a relationship is his job.

When a man identifies a woman to be the object of his desire, he will work passionately to secure her for his very own.

The chase is the time *before* sexual involvement, when a man seeks a woman's company and amorously pursues her favor. It is also the time frame during which he:

A. Evaluates, understands and appreciates the woman he is dating

B. Forms an emotional attachment to her

A Man Needs Time to Fall in Love!

Rita, a good friend of mine, was an attractive 31-year-old widowed flight attendant. She met Steve, a divorced senior captain, on an overseas flight to Rome. He was stationed in Atlanta; she lived in Minneapolis-St. Paul.

When Rita and Steve landed in Rome they decided to share a taxi to the hotel and meet later for drinks in the lobby bar. Drinks turned into a romantic dinner. The romantic dinner ignited an evening of passionate kissing, and the return flight home was full of anticipation of what was yet to come.

The following week, Steve called Rita saying he wanted to see her again. That's all it took. Rita booked an immediate flight to Atlanta, sealing her fate before ever putting a foot on the plane. When Rita returned home, she reluctantly told me about her weekend with Steve:

Because Steve had a teenage son living with him, he could not invite Rita to stay at his home, so he reserved a hotel room for her. Upon arriving at the Atlanta airport, she begrudgingly caught a taxi to the hotel to wait for Steve. Long story short, Rita spent her anticipated weekend in a hotel room in bed with Steve, getting only an occasional glimpse of downtown Atlanta when they went out for dinner. At the end of each evening, Steve returned home to his son.

Steve never called Rita again. *Why would he?* **She** did all the work. **She** gave in to sex too soon. **She** tolerated his inhospitable behavior.

In the beginning Steve was quite smitten with Rita, and she was bubbling over because a senior captain pilot was expressing an interest in her. In all probability, had she allowed him to do the pursuing, he may have developed feelings for her.

Rita wouldn't admit it, but she deeply regretted having casual sex with Steve. "No big deal" she said flippantly. "It was a fun weekend. If he calls—he calls. If he doesn't— it's no biggie."

Who does she think she's kidding? What she's really feeling is: "If only I had done things differently, Steve might be flying in this weekend to see me."

It is the *allure of sex* that inflames a man's desire to pursue a woman. But . . . when a woman gives in too soon, he may lose interest in her, as well as his motivation for the chase.

Men want what they think they can't have and will go after it to prove their masculinity.

Ron, a divorced 54-year-old auditor: "I want a woman to withhold sex until the time is right. I want her to keep her standards high, give me a challenge and keep me in line. That's what makes me even more determined to have her for my very own. The catch is—while she's holding out—I'm busy falling in love. That's when the time is right for a woman to commit to me on a deeper level."

A Woman's Job Is to Put on the Brakes

A woman needs to feel loved and valued by the man with whom she is sexually intimate. She wants assurance that he is trustworthy and that he will remain committed to their relationship—*after they have sex*. The best time for a woman to develop trust for her man, and know that he is on the same page—is *prior* to sexual involvement.

The chase is a woman's golden opportunity to:

A. Evaluate, understand and learn to trust the man she is dating

B. Experience a man's ardent desire for her, and feel wanted, valued and safe *before* they have sex

When a woman has sex **before** she has fully embraced a man's regard for her, she may regret her decision and doubt her self-worth. It's no surprise then that the man loses interest in her and abandons the pursuit.

In the words of the infamous Camille, "When a man catches the squirrel too soon, he quits trying to impress a woman. That's when the gifts get smaller, the dinners get cheaper, and ya' can't get your yard done anymore!"

Girlfriends! *WAKE-UP, WISE-UP* and *STOP* giving bits and pieces of your minds, bodies and souls to men who are not deserving of your love and affection.

Eventually Rita did come around to discussing the demise of her short-lived relationship with Steve.

Rita, "The part that hurts the most about Steve was knowing that in the beginning he really liked me—but I screwed it up. I didn't let him pursue me, I was nonchalant about his rude behavior in Atlanta and I caved in to sex way, way too soon.

What I should have done was invite Steve to come to St. Paul, or tell him that I was busy and offer to go for a visit in a couple of weeks. I am sure if I hadn't appeared so anxious, he would have booked my flight, picked me up at the airport, offered me a guest room in his home, and shown me the time of my life in Atlanta. Even then, I should have postponed the sex until I knew him better. If I could turn back time—I would!"

Like it or not, it's a woman's job to *put-on-the-brakes* when a man is moving too fast *sexually*. It is her responsibility to monitor the sexual progress of the relationship and stay in control of her conduct while curtailing his advances.

It tells the man that she respects herself, she values her body and, if he wants the relationship to continue, it will require his attention, respect and commitment.

Premature Sex Skews Reality

Sex is a heavy-duty, mind-altering drug. It changes the focus of an immature relationship. It distorts the interpretation and temperament of a developing relationship. It skews the reality of an undeveloped relationship. Sex, or the *"desire-for-it,"* can cause a person to think, act and behave differently from the way she (or he) did before sex became an important factor.

Another girlfriend bites the dust:

Janie was a 45-year-old divorced business owner; Paul was seven years older, handsome, intelligent, successful and worldly.

He was generous, adoring and intuitive to her every need. After two months of dating Paul, she had yet to have sex with him, but the lure of romantic dinners, intimate conversations and gifts finally convinced her to go on vacation with him.

Paul booked an extravagant trip to Las Vegas, complete with all the frills of a limo, five-star hotel, the finest restaurants and headliner shows. She was impressed and she felt ready to commit to him in a sexual way. Before going to Las Vegas, she insisted that he be tested for sexually transmitted diseases.

The "Desire-For-Sex" Distorts Reality

It's funny how the mind works. One minute Janie was adamant about waiting for his test result for STD's, and the next minute, after making plans for the trip, sharing a bottle of wine and his offer to use a condom, she caved in to a night of passionate lovemaking. But Janie felt okay about it because she was sure he was the right man for her.

Two nights later, Paul called, saying he needed to talk. "I have genital herpes," he said. "I know that I should have told you before now, but I haven't had a breakout in ten years and I didn't think it was a problem."

Prematurely Sleeping With a Man Can Cause a Woman to Lose Her Ability to Reason.

At first Janie was stunned . . . then frightened . . . and then angry beyond words. "How could he keep this vitally important information from me?" she thought.

She broke off the relationship with Paul, not because he was a herpes carrier, but because he knowingly took away her right to make an educated decision about her health, welfare and future. He put her at risk of contracting an incurable disease!

Janie later realized that Paul's seductive, romantic style had turned all of her good intentions to mush. She started out dating him using care and discernment, and she thought that her eyes were wide open . . . but Paul had literally "charmed the pants off her."

Janie's relationship with Paul ended in an abrupt rude reality that came with a frightening lesson. She learned that the lure-of-sex can be a mind-altering force. Premature sex can be a serious health threat, as well as distort the reality of who a man truly is and the relationship that he is offering.

Delay and Postpone Sexual Involvement Until the Right Man Comes Along

To evaluate a man accurately, a woman must keep *a clear head.* That's not going to happen if she sleeps with him in the early stages of dating. Sex can overpower her ability to make rational and wise decisions. It can cause her to sugar-coat and deny the worst of character flaws and bad behavior in a man.

Bad Choices Create Bad Feelings Within.

When a woman repeatedly accepts a dysfunctional man into her life . . . *a man who is less than what she wants and deserves . . . the man is not the problem*, regardless of his shortcomings. The problem lies within *her* low esteem issues, *her* low standards, and *her* unwillingness to wait for the Right Man.

Often times a woman will succumb to a man's seduction to fill her own emotional void . . . or to gain his acceptance. But after she has sex with him and the relationship does not move forward (*or* ends abruptly), she feels mistrustful, deceived and devalued. Then she asks herself, *"Did I do the wrong thing? Does he still respect me? Will I ever hear from him again?"* These are the thoughts that fuel a woman's low self-esteem.

Granted, there are women who are comfortable with having casual sex. But—most of the women that I know are profoundly affected when they give themselves sexually to a man. I call it—soul-ties. A woman gives her body, but it's really her soul that she is sharing.

Sex with the Wrong Man can lower a woman's self-worth, and if repeated enough, will cause cumulative emotional damage.

Holding Out Can Be A Good Thing

It is a "valid dating maneuver" for a woman to keep a man *waiting* for and *wanting* the squirrel until she knows with whom she's getting involved. Withholding sex is not manipulation and control . . . *Au contraire!* This is a woman who is protecting **her own best interest!**

Withholding Sex is A Valid Dating Maneuver.

How long should a woman wait before having sex with a man?

Never consider having sex with a man without first discussing *safe sex!* Don't have sex until you feel emotionally and physically secure with a man. Other than that, sex is an extremely personal decision that has no hard-and-fast rules.

However, if you experience the following, you might want to reconsider your dating sexual behavior:

- You have a pattern of having sex too soon.
- You feel regret after having sex.
- You wind up having sex with the *Wrong Man.*
- Men seem to lose interest and stop calling you after you've had sex with them.

If you've ever awakened next to a man, singing . . .
"A-B-C-D-E-F-G" . . . and then said,
"Oh shit, now I remember . . . his name is George!"
you may want to rethink your dating behavior.

A man needs time to fulfill his role as a suitor and to develop romantic feelings. A woman needs time to trust a man and feel that she is an important part of his life. *How long should a woman wait before having sex?* The longer the better because sex is more important the *very first time!*

Warning! Warning

Be aware and protect yourself from men whose
sordid challenge is to score a sexual conquest with
the women who cross their paths. TAKE HEED and
STAY CLEAR of these self-gratifying predators.
Their unfair, unsafe and harmful
behavior will only bring you sorrow and regret.

Loss of Mystery

Ahh! . . . Anticipation! Who can forget the excitement of planning to buy their first new car, their first new home, or of landing their first real job? And who can forget the first time they fell in love, the first time they had sex, walking down the aisle to say "I do," or the birth of a child. What is it that makes these experiences so memorable? And why do we, as women, get the feeling of "butterflies" in our stomachs before the first date with a handsome man, in the midst of a new exciting romance, or before the first trip with a new romantic interest? It's called euphoria: the anticipation of the unknown and the promise of a dream come true.

"Anticipation, Anticipation. Is makin' me late; Is keepin' me waitin'," sings Carly Simon. Girlfriends, keep your guy waiting for your intimate secrets, deepest desires and most importantly, sex with you!

I have already stated the adverse consequences of premature sex in a newly developing relationship. I have said that men are hunters; they love the challenge of the chase, but when a woman ends the chase too soon by becoming sexually involved, his interest may dwindle, even die.

The allure of a woman's mystery is a powerful dating aphrodisiac.

Sex is not the only way a woman can lose her mystery. Her tendency to divulge everything about herself during the early stages of dating dilutes her attractiveness and allure. She professes her secret hopes, needs and desires; she discloses the sordid history of her past relationships, or she shares the personal details of her slovenly habits, illnesses or dysfunctional personality. She even admits to her sagging financial condition. Give her another martini and she may tell her date that her ex-boyfriend paid for her nose job and butt lift. Bottom line: A woman who gives up her feminine mystique by *telling all too soon* can lose a man's interest.

Why does a woman reveal embarrassing information about herself so freely and quickly? Conversational silence can be an uncomfortable monster. Oftentimes, an insecure woman will attempt to fill the void of silence by impulsively sharing the intimate details of her life. True, a woman eventually needs to share the majority of important information regarding her past, present and even future; however, appropriate timing is crucial in keeping a man's interest.

Rick, a 48-year-old dermatologist: "For me, a woman's feminine mystique is all about not knowing what she is going to say or do next. It's expecting her to do the unexpected. It's her off-the-cuff humor. It's when she surprises me with basketball tickets or a tantalizing note she leaves in my apartment to greet me the next morning. She's unpredictable . . . not in the unreliable, unstable sense, but in a way that stimulates and intrigues me. She is confident, self-reliant and powerful because she enjoys her own life, friends and interests and is not always available. However, she lets me know that she wants me in her life *when* it fits into her demanding schedule. This kind of mystery always gets a man's attention!"

Ginger gave up her mystique on the very first date. Ginger and Lonnie met on the internet, emailed one another for a month, and then meet at Starbucks for coffee. Lonnie was the cute blonde boy-next-door type and Maggie was wildly attracted to him the moment she set eyes on him. Two cups of coffee later, she anxiously began to reveal the dirty laundry of her past two divorces, a costly failed business venture, trouble with her children at home, and oh yeah . . . she got drunk and threw up at her girl-friend's Friday night. When Lonnie first saw Maggie, he was impressed by her tall, well-groomed and friendly presence. Thirty minutes

When a Woman's Mystery Dissipates, So Does the Magic of the Chase.

later, after listening to her blab her problems, his interest turned to concern and disinterest. *Hey Maggie*, next time zip it.

Some information is vital at the beginning of a relationship. Is he (or she) married or in a committed relationship? Is he separated from his wife and waiting for a divorce? Is he recently divorced? Has he recently broken a long-term relationship? It's important to know if someone is on the mend. However, some issues should be shared only after a mutual interest has been established. For instance, in the beginning of a relationship don't blurt it out if:

- You've had a facelift, breast implant, Botox or Restylane injections and you have future plans for veneers and a tummy tuck.
- You're a spendaholic (he'll find that one out soon enough without you telling him).
- Your bank account is overdrawn and you're prone to bounce checks.
- You're an unwed mother and can't find your child's father.
- You've had a lesbian experience or a three-way sexual encounter.
- You can't collect child support from your ex-husband.
- You have a vibrator or battery-operated boyfriend.
- You cheated on your boyfriend or husband.
- You've had multiple divorces.
- You used to weigh 300 pounds.
- You want to get married.
- *Did I leave anything out?*

However, as soon as you know mutual romantic feelings are developing, it is time to discuss following:

- Negative financial situations that could impact the other person's established finances.
- Pertinent information about children that could affect the future of a relationship.

- Past or ongoing alcohol, drug or sexual addictions and other compulsive disorders.
- Safe sex and/or sexually transmitted diseases.
- Past arrest records or imprisonment.
- Any other issue that could come back to haunt you and impact your partner's trust or the quality of his life in the future with you.

Sharing the intimate details of one's life is relative to the situation and your own personal belief system. Just remember, a little mystery is sexy . . . but evasive, dishonest, scheming behavior—*is foul play!*

The Talented, Mysterious Annie

Too much information too soon, will leave nothing to challenge a man's intellect, curiosity or dating prowess. Whereas, a woman of few words can be extremely intriguing.

It is the anticipation . . . waiting for unknown . . . that keeps a man's adrenaline going and keeps him in hot pursuit.

When it comes to men, the most alluring, enticing woman I've ever known was my friend Annie. She teetered on the edge of aloofness, but was friendly and sociable. She appeared confident, laughed easily and softly, and her relaxed, mischievous smile seemed to beckon to men. One night, while we were at a night club, I watched the effect Annie had on a handsome man who was showing an interest in her. He wasn't quite sure what Annie was thinking . . . but he was intrigued, and he wanted to know more about her.

Annie: "The fact that I hold back and don't give everything away is what makes me mysterious, and therefore intriguing. It's human nature to have curiosity; my mystery keeps a man guessing and challenges him. And the challenge inspires him to chase me. In other words don't spell it out for him but become a fascinating puzzle that he needs to solve—one piece at a time."

A woman's mystery puts a man at a slight disadvantage in a new relationship *(that's not a bad thing)* causing the *hunter* in him to work harder to prove himself worthy of her interest.

Patrick, a 37-year-old restaurant owner: "When I met Tara, I thought she was the most captivating woman I had ever met. She wasn't the best looking woman in the room, but her aura of mystique and self-confidence caught my attention. We began to date, and she always seemed be on top of her game. She loved her job, spent quality time with her children, had great friends and attended social events. She was interesting; she was in control of her life and contributed to the overall quality of our relationship. I was delighted to be a part of her world."

Appropriate Mystery

Being mysterious is not the same as being dishonest and deceptive.

After a month of dating Garrett, our relationship seemed to be progressing nicely. I liked him and I was certain he liked me, as well.

Four weeks into dating him I went to an out-of-town church retreat weekend by myself. I told Garrett that I was going out of town, but on the advice of a girlfriend, I purposely withheld the trip's details. "Leave him guessing," she said. "He may think that you're dating someone else and it will only make him want your more." Wrong! Wrong! Wrong! I never heard from Garrett again. Sensing that I screwed up, I called him when I returned home and left him a message saying, "Missed you. Want to see you. Give me a call." Garrett never returned my call. The lesson I learned was that a little feminine mystery is intriguing—but don't play jealous mind-games if you want a man to trust you.

Mystery Tips

- Foremost, a woman's mystique is always greater *before* sexual involvement with a man.

- Always be honest and sincere, yet light-hearted; the time to share the serious aspects of your life can vary, but before you do, you first need to trust a man.

- Keep the conversational spotlight on the man and away from yourself; encourage him to talk about himself by asking him questions.

- Discussing his career, current news, movie and book reviews and sport events will help you fill the conversational void.

- Don't always be available. It's okay to leave out the details of your life, but don't be evasive or dishonest; a man will sense your manipulation and resent you.

- Be aware that women who have never established healthy boundaries, or who need a man's approval, are prone to *tell all*. Focus on his need for approval and admiration, which will inadvertently boost *your* confidence and self-esteem.

- A woman with outside interests will be more appealing to a man, whether it be her career, hobbies, personal or social interests. And a woman who is financially capable of taking care of herself is, in a man's eye, the "Diva of Mystery."

- Finally, it is always best to err on the side of honesty than to trap a man with tricks or lies.

Never Hunt a Dead Animal

Never, never, never hunt a *Dead Animal!* *What is a Dead Animal?* you ask.

He is a man who is mentally, emotionally, physically or financially unavailable to participate in a loving, healthy, stable relationship. He's either an alcoholic, sportsaholic, workaholic, gambler, womanizer, abuser, drug addict, sex addict, con-artist, criminal, or he has a commitment phobia. He may have emotions . . . but he's already married . . . and *they belong to his wife.*

A Dead Animal is a man who takes great interest in his own hobbies, friends, job, comforts, concerns and problems—*but*, he takes *little or no interest* in the things that are important to the woman in his life.

He'll happily drink beer, golf, hunt or play cards with his buddies 24-7 . . . but when it comes to a moment of meaningful conversation with his *girlfriend* or *wife*, he turns a deaf ear. He's considerate, patient and understanding in the workplace . . . but when dealing with her problems, he alienates her with his unsympathetic comments. He loves to spend money on his hobbies, tools and cars . . . but the last bouquet of flowers or piece of lingerie she received was after the first time she slept with him.

*A Dead Animal brings precious little to the relationship table
and if you stay with him long enough,
he will suck the love, life and spirit right out of you.*

The Tell-Tale Signs of a Dead Animal

A *Dead Animal* is not always easy to detect. He appears to be a living, breathing creature. He seems to be charming, trustworthy, considerate and generous. You may even be thinking, *"He could be the Man-of-My-Dreams."* But as we peel away his layers and take a closer look, the tell-tale signs of a highly dysfunctional man become obvious.

ॐ ♥ ॐ

Edward is a real enigma. One minute he's expressing his adoration and passion for his girlfriend Wanda. An hour later he is an unpredictable, ill-tempered, controlling tyrant. And if she protests and calls attention to his hurtful behavior, he justifies it, points an accusing finger and denies it. Dazed and hurt, Wanda wonders what brought about the drastic change in his personality.

Don't fall prey to the influence of A Dead Animal's charm . . . the moment he gets you, he will reveal his nasty, bad-tempered self.

❧ ♥ ❧

Everyone loves Tommy . . . especially the women. In the office he is an even-tempered, confident, successful businessman. In a social setting he is considerate, charming and funny, a real "good egg" as they say. But when the sun sets and he unwinds in the privacy of his home, his wife Barbara knows him as an insensitive, withdrawn, uncommunicative recluse.

❧ ♥ ❧

Jerry's specialty is double talk, lies and empty promises. When Diana first met Jerry, he bragged about his successful career as a corporate executive, his expensive homes in Los Angeles and Chicago, his Harvard degree, his diplomatic connections—yadda, yadda, yadda— you get the picture. Five months later Jerry's phony facade began to crumble. Quite by accident, Diana discovered that his "expensive" home in L.A. was a tiny corporate apartment; he had lost his job as a company "manager," and moved back to Pittsburgh to live with his Momma while he looked for work.

A Dead Animal Is a Waste of Good Oxygen.

❧ ♥ ❧

Short and simple—a *Dead Animal* is a **bad** relationship risk. You can kick him. You can shake him. You can threaten and scream at him—but you can't make a *Dead Animal* participate in a relationship in a meaningful way. He's **dead, dead, dead** and you'll wear yourself out trying to bring him to life.

Dead Animal Warning

If you find a Dead Animal who can be
a good male friend—go for it.
But don't get intimately involved with him and
don't try to fix him up with your girlfriends.

To Change the Type of Man You Attract, You Must First Change Yourself

Why does a woman repeatedly commit herself to men that are known to be bad relationship risks? Because it's her "Comfort Zone." She is comfortable in the unhealthy relationships that mirror her own bad behavior, emotional hang-ups and the codependency issues of her past. In other words, if her father was an uncommunicative, punishing kind of guy—that might not feel so bad in a husband. Or, if as a young girl, she witnessed her father abusing her mother—she might overlook the occasional times that her boyfriend decides to slug her.

A Woman Who Knows Herself Becomes More Selective About the Men She Allows in Her Life.

A woman will continue to make bad choices as long as the bad behavior of her past is her point of reference. Once she is able to pinpoint, feel and heal the damage of her dysfunctional past, she can then starting correcting her bad behavior and she will be more apt to wait for a healthier man.

The Only Person a Woman Can Fix is Herself!

Libby, "I grew up in an uncommunicative family; my dead animal addictions are men who refuse to communicate or work on our relationship problems.

I knew that a perfect relationship was a myth and that it takes work from both sides to keep it on track; when I met Kevin I felt confident we could make that happen. In the early intimate stages of our relationship he seemed quite willing to express his love for me, but as time went by the sex became less frequent and so did his desire to talk. A year into our relationship Kevin withdrew into himself and his hobbies and refused to discuss our problems. I couldn't even get a decent argument out of him.

Identify Your Dead Animal Addictions and— Get Rid of Them

Eventually I went to counseling by myself. I cried. I screamed. I let go of my painful past, and I learned how to verbally express my feelings. When I completed counseling, I realized I had outgrown Kevin.

I broke up with Kevin and I moved on to look for a man who was capable of communicating on a caring level. I told myself that never again would I have a dead animal in my life.

ﾟ ♥ ﾟ

If you hear a tiny, desperate voice screaming from within: *"Beware! Danger! Dead Animal ahead!"* **Take heed.** It's your intuition trying to save you from a Dead Animal who will eventually make you feel dead inside too.

Recognizing *When* to Move On

*H*opefully, I have warned you about the traits and behavior of a *Dead Animal*, and you will be able to avoid a romantic entanglement with one. But if I am too late, and you are already in an unhappy relationship, and uncertain as to what to do—*read on.*

Women Think If They Can Change the Man, They Can Save the Relationship

When it comes to a dysfunctional man, a woman wants to dissect him, analyze him, categorize him and agonize over him—*over and over again.* It's her way of trying to understand what's **wrong** with her man, what's **wrong** with their relationship and **what** can she do to fix it?

A Woman Keeps Trying to Fix Her Dead Animal, But the Problem is . . . He's Permanently Broken.

The problem is: You can't change the spots on a *Dead Animal* and you can't change the harmful behavior of a dysfunctional man. He is what he is, and he always will be. That is, **unless** a bolt of lightening intervenes, causing him to stop drinking, get appropriate medication, or seek counseling for his emotional problems. But until that happens, she will live in hell with him and his self-destructive issues.

Set your limits on how much time you are willing to waste on trying to fix your relationship with a dysfunctional man.

Granted, there is some dysfunctional behavior with which we women are willing to live. Likewise, men are willing to accept some of our bad behavior . . . and that's reasonable. But *staying* with a dysfunctional man in a dead-end relationship that continually assaults a woman's spirit is a *tragic waste of life.*

It took years for Nadine to get a divorce from Wendell, a man who had long ago proven himself to be untrustworthy, adulterous and physically abusive. A year after her divorce, unbelievably, she was considering reconciliation with him.

At Wendell's invitation, Nadine went to his home to talk, they had a few drinks and then he erupted into his usual combative rage. "Look at what he did to me," Nadine sobbed as she rolled up her sleeve to reveal a bruise, so large and so black it made me gasp.

"He's hit me before." Nadine whined. "This time I swore out an assault warrant on him. Now he's calls me ten times a day, begging me to drop the charges, saying he still loves me and wants me to go back to him. I'm so confused; I don't know what to do because I still love him."

"Confused about what?!?!" I screamed. "Don't you understand if you go back to him, he'll kill you? If not physically—certainly emotionally!"

For years Nadine had made excuses for Wendell's steroid drug and alcohol addictions. For years she endured his infidelity and abuse. For years he kept her isolated from her friends and family. It was only when she discovered that he had leased an apartment for another woman, that she finally got fed up and filed for divorce. She started the healing process, renewed her lost friendships and even managed to scrape up enough money to buy a small gift boutique. Just when she seemed to be getting her life together . . . Wendell slithered up on her doorstep. It's hard to believe that she would even consider going back to a man who would eventually destroy her.

Some Relationships Are Wrong From Inception, Others Erode With Time

Everyone agrees that most relationships start out with a love that is strong and a future that is bright, but time and life's circumstances can alter even the best of intentions. Passion becomes apathy. Love transforms into resentment. Even the loyalty and commitment that was once pledged is sometimes exchanged for an extramarital affair.

Truly, I pity women who remain in an unhappy marriage out of commitment and loyalty. I was never one to live my life as a corpse.

I was very much in love with Robert and married him after only eight months of dating. All in all, he was a good man, dependable and honest, and while we were dating he was attentive, communicative and fun-loving. But four months after we were married, he became hyper-critical and verbally and sexually withdrawn. It was as if we went to bed one night and the next morning I woke up with a different man.

For the next ten years I begged Robert to pay attention to me and when that didn't work, I strove to need less and less from him. When he refused to go to counseling, I went by myself. I used my girlfriends as a source of companionship, and then I finally I buried myself in my career, all of which worked for me for a long time.

At the end of the ninth year, I felt hollow inside. If only Robert had met me half way, we could have made our marriage work. But he wouldn't, he didn't and he couldn't and my love for him slowly drained away. I had to decide whether to stay or to go.

It was loyalty and commitment that had kept me with Robert all those unhappy years, and it was my feelings of guilt and failure that kept me from leaving him. But I could no longer bear the thought of living in a loveless, lifeless void, so I asked Robert for a divorce.

Regrets? Yes, I wish I had paid attention to the early warning signs while we were dating that Robert was the silent brooding type. I wish I had bit the bullet in our first year of marriage, admitted my mistake, cut my losses and moved on before ten more years had passed by.

Feel the Pain Now—Or Feel the Pain Later

Hurt as it May and Hard as It is to Accept There Are Some Relationships That Are Doomed.

What hurts more in a bad relationship? *To stay . . . or to go?*

A woman will waste years of her life trying to fix a relationship with a dysfunctional man. Who can blame her for hoping that the man she loves will stop criticizing, berating, arguing,

lying, womanizing, cheating, being unemployed, withdraw-
ing, hitting, drinking, drugging and gambling? No matter *how
bad* a *bad* relationship is, it hurts to end it if you still love your
partner. Nevertheless:

- If you continually find yourself feeling unloved, needy,
  jealous, insecure, invalidated, crazy, unsafe, frightened,
  distraught or depressed;
- If your man refuses to communicate or get help for the
  problems in your relationship;
- If he refuses to take responsibility for his harmful
  behavior, and instead denies it, minimizes it or turns the
  blame on you;
- If he promises to change *but* he never does . . . *it may be
  time to think about your life without him in it!*

*The question is: do you want to feel the pain NOW—
or do you want to feel the pain LATER . . .
because sooner or later, a bad relationship has a
way of ending with a broken heart.*

WAKE-UP Call!

If any of the following describes you, you need to re-evaluate
your relationship:

- If you're in a serious relationship and are the only one
  who wants a commitment, quit wasting your time and—
  move on!
- If you're dating a single man, but he neglects to tell you
  he's in another relationship he's a liar and you need to
  deep-six him!

- If you're dating a man and you find out that he is married—and he didn't tell you—he's a two-timing liar—*bury him!*

- If he talks negatively about his ex-wife or past girlfriend, he's harboring anger and resentment, all of which you will soon be the next recipient—*run for the nearest exit!*

- If he's not calling you anymore, that means he's not interested in you anymore, which means he's not thinking about you anymore. *Stop* thinking about him and—*move on with your life.*

- If he's seeing someone else, that means he is interested in someone, but it is *not you—take a tropical vacation!*

- If he can't hold down a job, doesn't pay his bills, can't save money—Oh, my God, did he just ask me for a loan?—*Show him the door!*

- If he is undependable or dishonest (overtly or by omission), or you catch him lying or cheating—*throw him overboard!*

- If he's emotionally and verbally abusive (e.g., hyper-critical, sarcastic, spiteful, discounting, blaming, accusing or demeaning) *he is unworthy of your loyalty.*

- If he is physically abusive, *he's a criminal and should go to jail!*

- If he has a harmful addiction (e.g., drinking, gambling, work, drugs, promiscuous sex) understand that his addiction controls him and he cannot control the addiction or its associated bad behavior. If he refuses to quit and get professional help—*vanish and never reappear!*

- If he makes you feel jealous or mistrustful by overtly flirting with other women, and then he tells you, "You are over-reacting"—*tell him to take a permanent hike.*

Once out of a bad relationship, you will only benefit if you stop making the same relationship mistakes.

NEVER is there a worthwhile reason for a woman to stay with a man who continues to destroy her spirit, dignity and feelings of self-worth. Not even for the sake of commitment, family ties, children, finance or position.

Change your lifestyle, your phone numbers and the locks on your house; hide your children, money, pets and jewelry; get support from your family and friends, and tell that lifeless, worthless Dead Animal to "MOVE ON."

Part Six

90-Day Dating Principles

"Choice, not chance, determines destiny."
—Anonymous

"The man that a woman chooses to become her life's partner can impact her more so than any other decision she can make.
—Nancy Nichols

90-Day Dating Plan

Psychologists theorize that it takes a year of dating before you can really know someone. They also caution that a couple should refrain from sexual involvement during that first year. In a perfect world that would be great. Realistically though, it is doubtful that will happen.

The *90-Day Dating Plan* is my adaptation of this theory, based on my personal experience and that of my esteemed friends. I hope it is helpful for you.

Enjoy, Explore and Evaluate the Man

Dating is a mathematical science. Somewhere between 30 to 90 days a man will, most often, *begin* to reveal his true self. A woman who reserves emotional and sexual involvement during that time can more clearly view a man's positive qualities, as well as his unacceptable, negative traits.

My girlfriend Debbie swears that a man will reveal his true nature sometime within the first three months of dating.

Debbie: "I want to know who I'm getting involved with

before I commit to intimacy with a man. I want to see how he interacts with his friends and business associates, how he treats money and how willing he is to spend it on our relationship. What his relationship is like with his children, family, and especially, how does he treat his mother? I want to know how he reacts to stress, how he behaves when he's angry. And when he gets angry is he forgiving or does he hold a grudge? Especially revealing is how does he behave after having a few cocktails? And did any of his behavior patterns contribute to the failure of his last relationship?

When I date a guy, I don't have expectations of him; I don't pressure him for a relationship, and I don't have sex with him. And then, just like magic, in the first ninety days when he gets comfortable with me, he will start to reveal his lousy attitude and foul behavior if he has them. And if he does, I will turn heel in my pretty little pumps and leave. It saves me from getting involved with sickos, felons and freeloaders."

I agree that it takes twelve months to really get to know a man. It takes four seasons—spring, summer, winter and fall—to experience the varying circumstances that can bring out the best and worst in a man. If only we women could wait that long.

Women are naturally slaves to their emotions and romantic longings. They are unwilling or unable to wait twelve months before committing to a man (and who can blame them?) But when they are hasty they may later discover they're in bed with *bad news*.

The "90-Day Dating Plan" is a short-range strategy that helps a woman avoid emotional involvement with the WRONG MAN.

The *90-Day Dating Plan* is targeted at the woman whose motivating force in life is to have a man. She tends to believe everything a guy tells her. She gives her heart and her body to a man she barely knows. And more often than not, she picks the Wrong Man. To this woman I say, divide the early stages of the dating process into emotionally manageable, bite-size time segments. *Slow down*, reserve judgment, resist emotional involvement and sexual temptation to give the man a chance to show you *who he really is.*

Some Women Do Not Know How to Separate the Bad Guys From the Good Guys.

The 90-Day Dating Approach:

1. Define and write down a man's qualities, standards and values that are important to you.

2. Keep your emotions in check while you look for a man with those qualities.

3. If a man turns out to be lacking the standards you require, back away before you become emotionally attached to an undesirable man.

30-60-90 Days to Evaluate the Man

Divide the first 90-days of dating into three 30-day dating segments.

Days 1 through 30: During the first thirty days get to know the man you are dating. It's nothing serious . . . just a month of fun, food and entertainment with a new friend. It is an opportunity for conversation over dinner, or an escort for the theatre or a party. Don't make snap judgments, and whatever you do, *do not project romantic thoughts of him into your future!*

Days 30 through 60: It's not unusual for romantic feelings to begin to develop after dating for thirty days. *But WAIT!* Has he said or done anything that has caused you a moment of concern? *No?* Then wisely proceed for thirty days more, digging deeper into the qualities, standards, values and *stability* of your man. Kissing is okay. *Sex is not.* Continue to look for any questionable behavior that might develop.

Days 60 through 90: It's the final thirty days. Maybe you stopped dating your man because there was no attraction for you, or he displayed unacceptable behavior. But if instead, you find yourself developing romantic feelings for him and there is no evidence of deception, bad behavior or addictions . . . you may want to consider the following:

- Is he worth more of your time, effort and attention?
- Is there a possible romantic connection in the future with him?
- Do you feel safe committing to him at a deeper emotional level?
- OR—is he only meant to be a friend?

The point is, if you've used your head instead of your "emotional appetite," you are in a much better position to make a sane, logical decision of whether to stay and pursue a romantic connection with this man—or, *cut bait and run.*

Remember, it's NEVER about what a man says.
It is ALWAYS about what he DOES.
Do his actions back-up his spoken word?

Time is relative. Dating a man twice a month will reveal precious little about him. On the other hand, dating him every weekend, plus a weeknight . . . and having frequent phone conversations in-between for several months, can give you the time you need to discover his true identity.

Remember, there is a difference between *judging* a man versus *assessing* his character; take the time you need to get the data with which to make a sound evaluation. Then *YOU* decide . . . is he your *Dream Man*—or is he the *Wrong Man?*

36
Fast Track to Finding the Right Man

*T*he quickest route . . . the *Fast-Track* . . . to finding the *Right Man* is to avoid wasting time on the *Wrong Man*.

A Good Looking Man May Not Be That Great on the Inside.

He's good looking, a sharp dresser and a real *s-m-o-o-t-h* talker. He's charismatic, well-positioned in life and he knows how to show a woman a good time. **Watch out!** This could be the man that will break your heart.

So easy is it for a woman to overlook a man's harmful behavior when it is camouflaged beneath flowers and gifts, expensive silk ties, and convincing verbage. She buys into his façade and falls quickly and madly in love with him, only to discover later that he is incapable of contributing to a meaningful relationship. He is the man for whom they coined the term—*an Empty Suit.*

My friend Lauren, a 43-year-old divorced real estate agent tells her story: "Rod was a 37-year-old divorced television executive, who had recently transferred to Chicago, my hometown. We met at a Christmas party. It was Rod's impeccable style that first caught my eye but it was his confidence, wit and personality that seriously got my attention.

Rod and I were immediately attracted to one another. We spent the evening laughing and talking; in two brief hours I was ready to take him home with me. The problem was that I found out that Rod was already involved in a seven-year relationship; the party ended and we went our separate ways.

Three months passed when quite unexpectedly I received an email from Rod. It read, *'Have been leasing an apartment since arriving in Chicago. I'm ready to purchase a downtown condo. Would you be available to show me properties?'* The next day I met Rod to discuss the search for his condo.

Rod told me he had broken up with his girlfriend, and for the next two months I showed him condos while he treated me to elaborate outings and dinners. He was the perfect Southern gentlemen. He dazzled me and my girlfriends with his flamboyant ways; he befriended my guy friends by buying them free rounds of drinks. Everyone who met him was impressed.

Rod eventually bought a condo, and I quickly fell in love with him. We got along perfectly together. Sex was incredible. My family and friends embraced him. I told everyone I had found the Love-of-My-Life.

It was exactly eleven months and twenty-nine days later, two days before celebrating our one year anniversary, that Rod sent me an unforeseen devastating email. In it he said, he adored and respected me—but *unfortunately*, he was not in love with me. He had set a mental time clock for falling in love, and when it didn't happen, his alarm went off. And just like that, in a cold, cryptic internet message—*he dumped me!*

I realize now that everything that Rod said and did was all for appearance. His mannerisms, generosity, even his impeccable dress, was his creation of a successful businessman, model boyfriend, chivalrous host and devoted father. Nevertheless, there were undeniable warning signs that this was not the case. He became unruly, critical and argumentative when he drank alcohol. He was belligerent with his 18-year-old daughter and I knew if he could talk to his daughter that way, he would one day do the same to me. I never heard from Rod again.

Rod was a peacock, a charmer . . . a phony in sheep's clothing. He had hood-winked me, fooled my family and friends, and then he cruelly crushed my heart. No matter how exquisitely tailor-made his clothing is, he will always be the man in an empty suit."

Judging a man's character with superficial information is risky business.

Settling for Less

When a woman can't find the *Right Man*, she will often settle for the *Wrong Man*. She yearns to be in a loving, caring, stable relationship . . . but as times passes, and the *Right Man* doesn't show up . . . she grows weary, lowers her standards and recklessly allows the *Wrong Man* into her life. Once she is committed sexually, she is no longer emotionally available to meet and date the *Right Man.*

∻ ♥ ∽

I told myself, no matter how cute, adorable, successful or tempting a guy might be, and no matter how much I liked him . . . if he exhibited hurtful, dysfunctional behavior ***I had to quit dating him!*** I just couldn't afford to waste another ten, five, or even one more year on the *Wrong Man.*

I was 43-years-old when I met Cory at a pool party. He was tall, handsome and divorced. He was an ex-state legislator, ex-Air Force fighter pilot, and an extremely successful business owner. But what I noticed most about Cory were his penetrating blue eyes and devilishly boyish smile. Cory o-o-z-e-d charm. You can imagine my astonishment and delight when he finagled my phone number from the hostess and called me at home that same night.

The abridged story is: I dated this tantalizing stud-muffin for three months, all the while being extremely careful to let my brain rule over my emotionally charged desires. Sure enough, sometime around sixty days of dating him, his bad boy ways began to surface. Yes, Cory was adorable, fun-loving and successful—but he was also an arrogant, unstable egomaniac who, when he drank, became surly, erratic and withdrawn. I knew that Cory would break my heart, and as much as I was reluctant to, I stopped dating him. After all, if I am emotionally and sexually unattached, I am free to keep meeting and dating men until I find the Right Man for me.

The Courtship Smoke Screen

Men are programmed to tell women what they want to hear. Men are the "experts of all explanations" for their bad behavior. It seems like it is their genetic encoding. It is our job to see through their smoke screen.

There was something about Ray that I just couldn't quite put my finger on.

Ray was the first man I dated after my divorce. We attended the same high school, and thirty years later I ran into him at church.

Dating Ray was easy. He was stable, spiritual and a perfect gentleman. He called me regularly and he took me to church on Sundays. He even fixed my leaking toilet. And with his extended social group, there were always friends to dine and have fun with. Ray looked, talked and acted like a "keeper." Nonetheless, I had an inexplicable nagging feeling that Ray was not all that he seemed to be.

*It was Saturday night and it was the first time I had been able to convince Ray to go to dinner with my friends. When the waitress came to take our orders, to my astonishment and without consulting me, Ray ordered an appetizer as my main entrée . . . then thirty minutes later he canceled my request for a glass of wine, telling me, "You don't have time to drink it." Ray selfishly could not spare an hour or a dollar to be with my friends, because he was in a hurry to get to his friend's house for a **free dinner**. The suspense was over— Ray was **cheap**!*

For three months there was something about Ray that I had not been able to pinpoint, but my patience finally paid off. There was no denying his unmistakably selfish behavior.

Looking back, I remembered several times when dining out, that he hadn't considered my preference when ordering a bottle of wine. At dinner parties he was the first to grab a doggie-bag so he could get the best and the most of the leftover food. Yes, Ray was a penny-pinching **tightwad!** *He talked like he wasn't and he tried to act like he wasn't, but in the end his actions gave him away. I knew if I continued to date him, and I wanted to eat, I had better bring my own credit card.*

Marcus was a nice-enough-looking divorced psychiatrist whom I dated. He was a member of a bee-bop dance club and we spent most of our dates dancing and socializing with his bee-bop friends.

Marcus, being the good psychiatrist that he was, knew how to have touchie-feelie conversations. Three months into dating him, I was considering a serious relationship. First, however, I needed to address a concern.

"Marcus," I said to him on the telephone, "I feel as if we always do the things that you enjoy, but when I ask to do something I enjoy—you blow it off."

Marcus, in his degreed wisdom, asked me a couple of canned, probing psychiatric questions and then he said, "Sounds to me like you still have anger issues with your ex-husband. You might want to re-visit your counselor!"

There it was—just like clockwork. The 90-day bad behavior benchmark. The first time I express my needs within the relationship—the psychiatrist goes psycho!

"Marcus," I said, "If there's one thing I've learned in all of my counseling, it's to trust my feelings and I'm going to do exactly that. I feel like I don't like you anymore and I feel like I never want you to call me again." And before he could draw another irrational breath, I slammed down the phone receiver.

I withheld emotional involvement; I stood up to Marcus' verbal manipulation and I cheerfully moved on to meet the Right Man.

My friend Harriet, a single 35-year-old sales professional, had been seriously dating Benjamin for two years, and she was ready to get married. When she mentioned this to Ben, he told her he couldn't get married until the last of his three children graduated from college.

"That's another five years," Harriet wailed.

Translation: Ben likes things the way they are and his children are a convenient excuse for not committing. He knew all along that he was not going to ask Harriet to marry him, but he enjoyed the perks of an intimate relationship, so he played it cool until Harriet finally pressed the issue.

Harriet, "I have wasted two years on that S.O.B. when I could have been looking for a man who wanted a permanent relationship."

Harriet's quandary at this point is: Does she want to wait five more years with the hope of marrying Ben? Or does she end the relationship now, chalk up the last two years to a learning experience, and start looking for the Right Man? My guess is, there were tell-tale signs all along that Ben was a non-committal kind of guy, but he masked his true intentions to keep Harriet in a dead-end relationship.

Who Is The Wrong Man?

Does he make you jealous? Does he make you wonder and worry? Does he make you feel irrational, illogical and angry? Does he make you doubt your intuition and common sense? Does he give you that yucky, sick feeling in the pit of your stomach? Does he make you reach for the Prozac? If so—he's the *Wrong Man* for you!

Does he make you feel CRAZY?

Be careful. Be very careful about the man with whom you choose to commit because if he's the *Wrong Man* he will waste years of your life, along with your chances of being with the *Right Man*.

90-Day Hunting List

How can a woman ever expect to find her *Ideal Man* if she doesn't *first* define who that man is?

The *"90-Day Hunting List"* is a detailed description of your *Dream Man*. It is a ledger sheet of checks and balances that will help you use your *left-brain logic*, rather than your emotionally charged *right-brain urges* when contemplating the qualities and compatibility of a man. More importantly, it *red flags* a man's character flaws and unacceptable behavior to help you avoid emotional and sexual involvement with the *Wrong Man*.

The "90-Day Hunting List" Sharpens a Woman's Man-Selecting Skills.

Keep an Open Mind

"Single gals are able to rule out seeing potential mates again after just three seconds of interaction, largely based on the person's looks. We suggest a second glance before opting out," says *Evolution and Human Behavior, Self Magazine,* June 2005.

Good Advice!

Impulsively judging a man to be the Wrong Man can let a Dream Man get away. Likewise:

Constantly hoping and looking for a better man to come along can cause a woman to reject a relationship with a wonderful man. I call it the "greener pasture syndrome." It is the infrastructure of a hyper-critical, judgmental attitude.

Things to Keep in an Open Mind:

1. Your goal is to find a man to whom you are intellectually, emotionally and physically attracted. Someone who is your equal. Someone who is capable of *co-contributing* to a loving, intimate, supportive, stable relationship.

2. Your "Hunting List" is not an exercise in judging and criticizing men. It is an exercise in evaluating and selecting the Right Man.

3. Prioritize the things you desire most in a man. Men will bring different contributions to the relationship table, so look for someone who has the majority of the qualities and traits that you want. The exception: You can't change the basic package, but you can help a receptive man make small personal improvements.

4. Be realistic. If your expectations are too high, no man can possibly meet them—lower them! If your expectations are too low, you will be sorry later—raise them!

5. Don't expect any man to bring about major improvements in your life. And certainly, don't expect a man to be your sole source of happiness!

6. Listen to your intuition. If you are not completely con-

vinced that a man is all that he seems to be . . . postpone emotional involvement and continue to assess his qualities and identifying his deficits.

7. Use your "Hunting List" to give you guidance, focus and moral support while you look for your Ideal Man.

Defining Your Man Goals

The Hunting List is your opportunity to define and describe your Dream Man. It is a checklist of the qualities, values, characteristics, personality traits, attitudes, background, hobbies, activities, profession, economic status and approximate physical appearance that exemplify your *Ideal Man.*

A Lioness Does Not Look for Her Soul Mate in a Baboon.

Is he corporate America wearing a power suit and alligator wingtips? Maybe he's a brainiac who swings a mean surgeon's scalpel. Or, perhaps he's the mild-mannered accountant who transforms into your favorite wine epicure and chef in the evening. Does he enjoy golfing, Harley motorcycles, traveling or antique shopping? Is he tall, dark and handsome . . . or is he graying, wearing bifocals and sporting love-handles? Does he love children, but hate cats and Guinea pigs? Are his best qualities dependability and stability, or is he an adventurous risk-taker? Who is *your* Ideal Man?

Equally important is being able to define a man's bad habits, character flaws and the unacceptable behavior that you absolutely refuse to live with.

Maybe you smoke and enjoy a good Vodka Gimlet . . . and you like a guy who feels the same way. Or, maybe you're a teetotaler who stopped smoking ten years ago, and you find both highly objectionable. One woman says, "No big deal," to a man's dirty automobile, three-day scratchy beard and tardiness . . . but another woman finds it all very unappealing. One woman's discard is another's woman's treasure.

Give a man time to reveal his true self; refer to your "Hunting List" often. Trust your intuition and guard your emotions until you are certain you are with the *Right Man*.

90-Day Hunting List

An Unwritten Goal Is Nothing More Than a Pipe-Dream.

Check the qualities and descriptions that are important to you in a man:

<u>Qualities</u>

☐ Adventurous
☐ Affectionate
☐ Ambitious
☐ Assertive
☐ Caring
☐ Conservative
☐ Communicative
☐ Creative
☐ Dependable

☐ Disciplined
☐ Easy-Going
☐ Energetic
☐ Friendly
☐ Generous
☐ Hardworking
☐ Honest
☐ Liberal
☐ Loyal

☐ Open-minded
☐ Optimistic
☐ Out-going
☐ Patient
☐ Reliable
☐ Romantic
☐ Stable
☐ Thrifty
☐ Trustworthy
☐ Understanding

Other Qualities:

_____   _____

_____   _____

<u>Important Values</u>

☐ Family
☐ Children

☐ Friends
☐ Animals

☐ Environment
☐ Philosophies

Other Values:

_____

_____

Interests

- Art
- Antiques
- Bicycling
- Boating
- Camping
- Cooking
- Dining Out
- Entertaining
- Exercising
- Flying
- Gardening
- Golf
- Hiking
- Hunting/Fishing
- Karate
- Horseback Riding
- Motorcycle Riding
- Mountain Climbing
- Movies
- Painting
- Photography
- Reading
- Running
- Scuba Diving
- Sky Diving
- Snow Skiing
- Stamps
- Tennis
- Theatre
- Travel
- Water Sports
- Writing

Other Interests:

_____

_____

Career

- Accountant
- Architect
- Armed Services
- Business Owner
- CEO
- Chef
- Computers
- Construction
- Doctor
- Engineer
- Entertainment
- Fireman
- Law Enforcement
- Landscaping
- Lawyer
- Managerial
- Musician
- Pilot
- Psychologist
- Sales
- Scientist
- Sports Industry
- Teacher
- Writer

Other Careers:

_____

_____

Religion

- Spiritual
- Not important

Religious Affiliation:

_____

- Worship
  - Weekly
  - Monthly
  - Occasionally

Education

☐ High School Grad   ☐ Technical Grad   ☐ Ph.D.
☐ College Grad   ☐ MBA

Physical Description

Nationality_____   Body Type_____
Height_____   Hair_____
Weight_____   Beard/Mustache _____

Other Physical Descriptions: Eye Color_____

_____   _____

_____   _____

It is equally important to define a man's
UNACCEPTABLE traits and bad habits.

Unacceptable Traits

☐ Argumentative   ☐ Dishonest   ☐ Manipulative
☐ Bad Tempered   ☐ Double-Talking   ☐ Narrow-Minded
☐ Bad Family   ☐ Insecure   ☐ Opinionated
   Relationships   ☐ Insensitive   ☐ Procrastinating
☐ Bad Relationship   ☐ Insincere   ☐ Selfish
   History   ☐ Impatient   ☐ Stubborn
☐ Controlling   ☐ Jealous   ☐ Uncommunicative
☐ Critical   ☐ Judgmental   ☐ Unreliable
☐ Deceptive   ☐ Lazy   ☐ Untrustworthy

Other:

_____   _____

_____   _____

<u>Unacceptable Habits</u>

☐ Bad Dental
   Hygiene
☐ Bad Personal
   Hygiene
☐ Bad Manners
☐ Smoker
☐ Cigar, Pipe

☐ Tobacco, Other
☐ Alcohol
   ○ None
   ○ Moderate
   ○ Excessive
☐ Drug Addiction
☐ Addictions, Other

☐ Dirty Automobile
☐ Messy Housekeeper
☐ Sloppy Dresser
☐ Objectionable Job
☐ Undesirable Pets
☐ Undesirable Family
   Members
☐ Undesirable Friends

Other:

_____

_____

_____

_____

Now weigh your information carefully and write: What do you like about him? What do you dislike and positively cannot live with?

Likes:

Dislikes:

Cut out the shopping list pages in this book, or use these examples as a guideline to create your own personalized list and refer to it often.

Journaling Shall Set You Free

Next to the *90-Day Hunting List*, the smartest thing a woman can do is to keep a journal about the man she is dating.

When a woman starts to fall in love, her tendency is to justify and downplay a man's misconduct. She loves him, she wants him . . . so she chooses to close her eyes to his harmful behavior in order to rationalize the relationship. Journaling documents the irrefutable facts that will help a woman cut through the fiction; with the facts emerges the truth. It is hard to deny a man's repeated bad behavior, as vague as it may seem, when it's staring you in the face in black ink.

In the Beginning a Woman Wants to Sugar-Coat a Man's Unacceptable Behavior.

Listen, observe and write. Document the events of your man's unseemly, inconsiderate or misleading behavior . . . *as they happen.* You can then validate that you weren't dreaming, you're not crazy and you weren't over-reacting.

Every time you have a disagreement or fight, be it large or small, write it down and date it. Record his words, actions and behavior, in addition to what you were feeling at the time.

Journaling Helps a Woman to Stop Second-Guessing What Her Intuition and Common Sense Already Know.

It may be nothing more than a couple working their way thorough a relationship curve. But if you discover that he has a negative pattern of relating that's turning your gut inside out . . . you need to back away and wait for a more suitable man to appear.

⁊ ❤ ↄ

Use the following pages to journal the events and behavior of the man you are dating . . . if you're doing it right, you'll need extra paper.

Learn to recognize and acknowledge when a choice is good or when it's bad. Heed your intuition, rely on your intelligence and clean-up your choices in men.

_____

_____

_____

_____

_____

_____

_____

_____

_____

_____

_____

_____

_____

_____

_____

_____

_____

_____

_____

_____

Gayle, "The first thing I look at are a man's shoes. If he can't take good care of his shoes . . . he's not going to take good care of me."

Allison: "I like construction workers. When I retire from teaching I'm going to go to work at Home Depot because I've heard you can find a lot of them there."

Lynnette: "There are some men that are just unacceptable to me. I can't find myself attracted to bald men. Maybe that's why I don't like to bowl."

_____

_____
_____
_____
_____
_____
_____
_____
_____
_____
_____
_____
_____
_____
_____
_____
_____
_____
_____
_____
_____

Do your personal work, define your Ideal Man and hold out for the *Right Man*. Then when you least expect it . . . suddenly and magically . . . the Love-of-Your-Life will appear right before your *Husband Hunting* eyes.

Final Thoughts

For me the self–improvement journey has been an ever-changing, often puzzling, painful learning process. It seems that just when I think I have *gotten it down,* I correct a negative attitude or behavior, or I disconnect with a negative entanglement, I am presented with yet, another difficult person, a challenging relationship or perplexing situation causing me to question my ability to be a good friend or caring partner. My confusion has been to identify the negative, hurtful behavior of myself and others. My struggle was knowing when to yield and trust someone, or instead, protect my feelings and beliefs with decisive personal boundaries—*without feeling guilty.* Eventually I learned to limit my association with hurtful, dysfunctional people and, in time, I discovered that attracting healthy, upbeat men required that I have a positive, healthy attitude as well.

Secrets of the Ultimate Husband Hunter was in its final stages of editing when I discovered a book that had a profound effect on my life. The book's central philosophy professes that *The Secret* to wealth, health, happiness, love and relationships lies in the "law of attraction." It is the power of our thoughts that form our entire life experience—*negative or positive!*

"Everything that's coming into your life you are attracting. You are the most powerful magnet in the Universe! . . . and this unfathomable magnetic power is emitted through your thoughts. It is scientifically proven that an affirmative thought is hundreds of times more powerful than a negative thought." Finally, *"If you think thoughts of love, guess who receives the benefits—you! The greater the love you feel and emit, the greater the power you are harnessing."* Rhonda Byrne (Editor), *The Secret,* 2006.

In *Secrets of the Ultimate Husband Hunter* you will find *The Secret* as it applies to the single dating woman. It is this: *Love-All-Men*; accept, appreciate and affirm a wider range of men, and in the same manner, love-all-people and you will be inspired to accept, love and honor *yourself.* This is the secret to living a confident, self-sufficient, powerful life.

A child is born with a perfect spirit; a newborn's mind is blank—*tabula rasa,* and is therefore open to receive any and all information to form her first thoughts. Her soul is pure and ready to experience its first feelings. As her impressionable mind, character and personality develops, it is filled with the influencing thoughts, beliefs and emotions of those around her and will affect her identity as adult—*good or bad.*

What if we could start life over? What if we could empty our think tanks, banish our negative mindsets and re-fill the newly created void with *only* positive, persistent, powerful thoughts? Would our present lives change dramatically? Would the constant frequency of positive thinking attract the circumstances, people and events that would create success, true love and good fortune?

Within the pages of *Secrets of the Ultimate Husband Hunter* you will find the influential attitudes and take-charge actions that will inspire you as a woman to tap into your innate personal power. What is your personal power? It is the culmination of your special gifts, unique personality and the inner strength that you *were born with*—but perhaps never developed. Tap into your personal dynamics and you will release your confident, self-reliant, alluring presence—the "law of attraction" that will get you the respect, love and happiness you so richly deserve in your lifetime.

Some women need to *toughen up,* some need to *soften up,* others need to *spruce up,* but largely, most of us need to *wise up.* There is always room for personal growth, and if you think you don't need it, you think you have completed it, or that the other person is always at fault, *you* are probably the very one who needs to change the most.

In the recommended reading section I have provided some of the books that I have enjoyed, benefited from and valued. Continue your personal work, create life-changing positive thoughts and remember, be careful . . . very, very careful of the man you point your bow and arrow at.

Happy hunting!

Appendix A: Memo to Men

Dear Male Readers,

I realize that many men will not understand, or possibly be offended by the title, *Secrets of the Ultimate Husband Hunter* and its symbols: hunt, bait, capture, snare, lure, etc. But I want to assure you, most women love and respect men, or we wouldn't want to capture one for our very own.

Secrets of the Ultimate Husband Hunter is the true story of a woman, whose deepest desire in life, was to attract, date and eventually *marry the Love-of-Her-Life*. Her problem was that she never developed good dating and relationship skills and habits; she was needy, self-conscious and insecure with men, and she always seemed to commit herself to the *Wrong Man*.

Then one day, quite by accident, she discovered a dating and relationship concept that changed the course of her life. She called it *Love-All-Men* which succinctly meant, "give all men a chance" to reveal their best qualities.

In the beginning her *Love-All-Men* dating strategy was a means-to-an-end to attract, meet and date men. Her theory was: She would get to know and appreciate a wide range of men, with the hope of one day meeting and marrying the *Love-of-Her-Life*. Then she realized that her incapacity to attract a Quality Man stemmed from her judgmental, disapproving attitude. Her inability to relate to men arose from her low self-esteem and lack of confidence. And her incapacity to wait for the Right Man came from her low self-worth.

Then the unexpected happened. As she ceased judging and criticizing men, she also ceased her harsh, unfair, self-condemnations. And as she dated a wider variety of men and learned to enjoy their company, she realized that she, too, was worthy of respect and appreciation. Her increased confidence and new inviting presence began to attract the interest of *Quality Men*.

Indeed, it was a serendipitous turn-of-events that transformed this needy, insecure, disapproving woman into an enticing, charming creature.

What are my credentials for writing this book? *I am that woman.*

I have spent the better part of my life in painful, dysfunctional relationships. I have dedicated years to reading self-help books and receiving professional counseling to help me understand and correct my negative attitudes. I have searched for years for the secret that attracts a *Quality Man* (a man who is caring, honest, supportive and loyal). I finally found my answers in the *Love-All-Men* approach.

Secrets of the Ultimate Husband Hunter is a dating, relationship, self-improvement book for the millions of divorced, widowed or single women who truly want a loving, caring, loyal man in their life but don't know how to find him. They are uncertain, insecure and mistrusting of men; disillusioned with dating; discouraged with the prospects of finding a *Quality Man*, or they repeatedly commit to the *Wrong Man*.

I have intentionally chosen words, phrases and comments to make my book lively, entertaining reading, while omitting others (on the advice of my male friends) you might otherwise find offensive. Most importantly, I have labored over the words that would relate with sincerity, the profound meaning of my personal dating and relationship experiences.

The hunting terms in my book are purposely and affectionately used in a pro-active manner to motivate a woman to take responsibility for the quality of her life. Fundamentally, my book says: *"Learn to appreciate the male gender. Clean up the nasty attitudes and dysfunctional dating behavior that has kept you from meeting, dating and keeping a man. Raise your standards and hold out for a Quality Man. Most importantly, learn to value, respect and take care of yourself!"*

The *Ultimate Husband Hunter* is actually the woman men seek. She has learned that to be with the *Right Man* . . . she must become the *Right Woman*. And so she did.

She learned to be open-minded about the men she meets and dates, she avoids the pitfalls of her past and the possible dysfunctional entrapments of her future, and she patiently waits for the *Right Man* to come into her life. Meanwhile, she is cognizant of her right to be treated with appreciation and respect. She has become the *Ultimate Woman* who is looking for her *Ultimate Man*.

So, my male readers, I encourage you . . . should you meet a woman who tells you, "I am a huntress, the goddess of love . . . I am the *Ultimate Husband Hunter*". . . gaze deep into her eyes and ask for her phone number. Because, my dear friends, you may have just met the *Love-of-Your-Life*.

Appendix B:
Recommended Reading

Dating and Relationships:

Deal Breakers: When to Work on a Relationship and When to Walk Away by Dr. Bethany Marshall. Simon & Schuster Adult Publishing Group, 2007.

Heartbreak-Free Dating: Stop Wasting Time in Dead-End Relationships and Find Everlasting Love by Jess Kennedy Williams. Palace Publishing, 2007.

Love Smart: Find the One You Want—Fix the One You Got by Dr. Phil C. McGraw. Free Press, 2005.

He's Just Not That Into You: The No-Excuses Truth to Understanding Guys by Greg Behrendt, Liz Tuccillo. Simon & Schuster Adult Publishing Group, 2004.

Men Are from Mars, Women Are From Venus: The Classic Guide to Understanding the Opposite Sex by John Gray, Ph.D. Harper Collins Publishers Inc., 2004

Men, Love & Sex: The Complete User's Guide for Women; Thousands of men confess their well-guarded secrets about how they think, feel and behave! by David Zinczenko, Ted Spiker. Rodale Press Inc., 2006.

Stop Getting Dumped! All You Need to Know to Make Men Fall Madly in Love With You and Marry 'The One' in 3 Years or Less by Lisa Daily. Penguin Group, 2002.

What Men Want: Three Professional Men Reveal to Women What it Takes to Make a Man Yours by Bradley Gerstman, Esq., Robert Seldes, M.D., Christopher Pizzo, CPA. Rodale, 2006.

Why Men Marry Bitches: A Woman's Guide to Winning Her Dream Man by Sherry Argov. Simon & Schuster Trade, 2006.

Spiritual and Self-Realization:

Battlefield of the Mind: Winning the Battle in Your Mind by Joyce Meyer. Joyce Meyer Trade, 2002.

Blink: The Power of Thinking Without Thinking by Malcolm Gladwell. Little Brown and Company, 2002.

Inside My Heart: Choosing to Live with Passion and Purpose by Robin McGraw. Nelson Books, 2006.

Live Your Best Life: A Treasury of Wisdom, Wit, Advice, Interviews, and Inspiration from O, The Oprah Magazine. Oxmoor House, 2005.

The Purpose Driven Life: What on Earth Am I Here For? by Rick Warren. Zondervan, 2002.

The Secret by Rhonda Byrne. The law of attraction: Everything that's coming into your life you are attracting. Atria Books/ Beyond Words Publishing, 2006.

Image:

Closet Smarts by Emily Neill. Body typing; flattering fashions that don't cost a fortune. Fair Winds Press, 2006.

Color Me Confident: Change Your Look—Change Your Life! by Veronique Henderson and Pat Henshaw. Colors, outfits, make-up and accessories that maximize your potential. Octopus Publishing Group, 2006.

Glamour's Big Book of Dos & Don'ts, Fashion Help for Every Woman by Cindi Leive and the Editors of Glamour. Penguin Group (USA) Inc., 2006.

The Power of Makeup; Looking Your Best at Every Age by Trish McEvoy, Simon & Schuster, 2003.

Laura Mercier; The New Beauty Secrets by Laura Mercier. Easy to follow step-by-step beauty advice to a flawless face. Simon & Schuster, 2006.

In Style: Secrets of Style: The Complete Guide to Dressing Your Best Every Day by the editors of *In Style*, Melcher Media, Inc., 2005.

The Lucky Shopping Manual: Building and Improving Your Wardrobe Piece by Piece by Kim France and Andrea Linett. Penguin Group (USA) Inc., 2003.

The Perricone Prescription: A Physician's 28-Day Program for Total Body and Face Rejuvenation by Nicholas Perricone, M.D., Harper Collins Publishers, 2004.

Additional Image Information:

Check out the magazine racks for a wealth of fashion, beauty and hair style information.

Schedule a personalized skincare and cosmetics consultation at any department store, retail Merle Norman Cosmetics store, or visit BeautiControl.com and MaryKay.com for an in-home consultation.

Refer to the yellow pages for an "image consultant" or "personal shopper" (fees may vary, as well as the level of expertise) or find a knowledgeable clothing salesperson at your favorite boutique.

Visit websites: The supply of image articles on the internet is endless. Use these key words for your online search: accessorizing, body type, color analysis, core wardrobe, cosmetics, eye glass frame shape, fashion, hair style, image consultants, image solutions, makeup artistry and skincare.

Appendix C: Source Notes

Chapter 5: Tips, Tactics and Techniques That Attract Men

31 *"The 'women who dare' are few; the women who 'stand and wait' are many."* Louisa May Alcott, *An Old-Fashioned Girl* (New York: A. L. Burt Company, 1870).

Chapter 9: Meeting New Men

56 *"52% of single women and 48% of single men have used a dating service—compared to only 8% a decade ago."* Survey of 38,912 singles conducted by, It's Just Lunch, dating for busy professionals, *NWA WorldTraveler*, 2006.

Chapter 21: Discovering Self-Confidence

121 *"Self-consciousness is the No. 1 enemy of self-confidence."* www.moreselfesteem.com, July 2006.

122 *"Learn how to keep the focus off yourself . . . make business con-*
tacts." www.more-selfesteem.com, July 2006.

Chapter 23: Smile!

131 *"Up to 93% of all communication is non-verbal."* The Positive
Way®, www.positive-way.com, December 2006.

131 *"60% of getting a positive message across is by way of body lan-*
guage." Albert Mehrabian Ph.D., *Psychology Today* (1968).

131 *"We have 10 to 30 seconds to make a favorable first impression."*
Ward-Green and Hill Associates Ltd., www.wghill.com, December 2006.

Chapter 24: Sprucing Up Your Curb Appeal

137 "79% of men on a first date take 15 minutes . . . " It's Just
Lunch, dating service, itsjustlunch.com, 2007.

139 *"Get Real."* Phillip C. McGraw, Ph.D. (Dr. Phil), *Life Strate-*
gies (New York: Hyperion, 1999) p 11.

141 "Women wear 20%" of their clothing 80% of the time."
www.OrganizeHome.com, Clothes Closets, December 2006.

Chapter 30: Survival Tips for the Needy, Fearful Woman

171 *"I didn't get married till I was 37 . . . "* Rachael Ray Show,
December 15, 2006.

Chapter 32: Loss of Mystery

185 *Anticipation*, Carly Simon, artist; Paul Samwell-Smith, pro-
ducer; Jacob Brackman, co-writer, (Electra Records, 1971).

Chapter 37: 90-Day Hunting List

220 *"Single gals are able to rule out seeing potential mates . . . a second glance before opting out."* Evolution and Human Behavior, *Self Magazine,* June 2005.

Final Thoughts

234 *"Everything that's coming into your life you are attracting."* Bob Proctor, Rhonda Byrne (Editor), *The Secret,* (Atria Books/ Beyond Words, 2006), p. 4.

234 *"You are the most powerful magnet in the Universe! . . . and this unfathomable magnetic power is emitted through your thoughts."* Rhonda Byrne (Editor), *The Secret,* (Atria Books/Beyond Words, 2006), p. 7.

234 *"It has been scientifically proven that an affirmative thought is hundreds of times more powerful than a negative thought."* Michael Bernard Beckwith, Rhonda Byrne (Editor), *The Secret,* (Atria Books/Beyond Words, 2006), p. 22.

234 *"If you think thoughts of love, guess who receives the benefits . . . power you are harnessing."* Rhonda Byrne (Editor), *The Secret,* (Atria Books/Beyond Words, 2006), p. 39.

Order Your Copies Today!

Secrets of the Ultimate Husband Hunter:
How to Attract Men, Enjoy Dating and Recognize the Love-of-Your-Life

Order at: **www.ultimatehusbandhunter.com**

To inquire about quantity discounts for bulk purchases,
please email:

info@epiphanyimprint.com